Glorious Life After Death

Glorious Life After Death

by

K.I. Isaac

D.K. Printworld (P) Ltd.
New Delhi

Cataloging in Publication Data — DK
[Courtesy: D.K. Agencies (P) Ltd. <docinfo@dkagencies.com>]

Isaac, K.I. (Kollamparambil, Iype), 1924 –
Glorious life after death / by K.I. Isaac.
xvi, 205 p., 22 cm.
Includes bibliographical references (p.)
Includes index.
ISBN 8124603758

1. Future life — Christianity. I. Title.

DDC 236.2 22

ISBN 81-246-0375-8 (PB)
First published in India in 2007

Published and printed by:
D.K. Printworld (P) Ltd.
Regd. Office: 'Sri Kunj', F-52, Bali Nagar
New Delhi-110 015
Phones: (011) 2545-3975; 2546-6019; *Fax*: (011) 2546-5926
E-mail: dkprintworld@vsnl.net
Website: www.dkprintworld.com

Dedicated to

the sacred memory of

my grandfather ***Iype Ithack,***
Kollámparambil, Valliangady, Kottayam (Kerala)
my grandmother ***Mariam,***

my father ***K.I. Iype,***

and

my mother ***Achamma***

who brought me up
from my infancy
in strict discipline of the Orthodox faith.

॥ मृत्योर्माऽमृतं गमय ॥

Mṛtyor ma amṛtaṁ gamaya

From death lead me to Immortality

Preface

If there is anything that is sure to happen in our life in this world, it is death. Generally no one likes even to think of death, because it is the end of this earthly life. Though the philosophy about it is *Mr̥tyor ma amr̥taṁ gamaya* meaning "All those who die are going to immortality," it is seldom understood. More grievous than that is the ignorance about the "Glorious Life After Death," for which we are created. Therefore most lives run on wrong tracks rather than leading to the true direction. Man is a triunity of Body, Mind and Spirit. It is only the physical body that perishes at death. The mind survives and accompanies the spirit, maintaining the fully spiritual personality as a human soul to live in eternity, communing with God. But to be in communion with the Holy God the human soul should have such meritorious graces earned in the given earthly life. In spite of the worldly biasing influences, there is an intrinsic God-consciousness in man irrespective of any religion or nationality, because he is a creation of God with a soul, in the image of God.

From very early days of human history the Holy Spirit of God had been inspiring the spirit of man in a Heaven-ward sway. The early Judeo-Christian scriptures and the Hindu Vedas, Upaniṣads etc. written millenniums ago by divinely inspired sages and religious prophets, are examples of Theophanic Revelations that brought religious harmony throughtout the world. But generally, man in his carnal nature in this earthly life, had been faultering in sinful ways, and became liable for condemnation. The wages of sin being spiritual death, to redeem human souls from spiritual death, it was God's plan to send a universal saviour to redeem humanity by means of a propitiating sacrifice.

This book is a humble effort to point out to that redeemer, who sacrificed himself in propitiation of the sins of the world. For each and every one, irrespective of caste, creed, nationality or religion, who approaches him in true faith and repentance, in this life before the Last judgement, he is the redeemer. He is the Lord Jesus Christ the Son of God, who incarnated as Son of Man and sacrificed himself on behalf of us for all our sins. By the merit of his sacrificial blood the way is opened for humanity before God the Father for acceptance in the sonship bequeathed through the Son of God, Jesus Chirst. With God the Father in Heaven is the Glorious Life After Death, as God's sons. I present this book to the world with prayer and hope that the readers may be inspired to lead a dedicated life to merit this Glorious Life After Death.

Bangalore
July 20, 2006

K.I. Isaac

Contents

1

Death

The Gateway to a Glorious Life in Eternity

Have you ever heard about "Life After Death" — a life of marvel that mortals are yet to make? Indeed as you all know, death is an event at which the soul of a human being leaves the mortal body in which it was abiding in human life. Therefore, let us start from the beginning of human life itself.

Human Life

God who is Love uttermost, sharing from His infinite spirit of Love, created man conferring on him a perfect individuality with a mind of free will, to love Him and for Him to love. The Holy Bible says that God formed the human body out of the dust of the ground He created, and He breathed His Life Giving Breath into his nostrils and thus the man came into existence as a living being of triunity of body, mind and spirit (Gen. 2:7). The Palmist says "For thou hast made him a little lower than the angels, and hast crowned him with glory and honour" (Psal. 8:5). Again: "I will praise Thee, for I am fearfully and wonderfully made; marvellous are Thy works; and that my soul knoweth right well" (Psalms 139:14).

God had prepared in advance the earth suitable for human habitation by providing atmosphere with oxygen in the correct proportion and pressure; the sky around it with sun, moon and stars to give light and to indicate day and night with accurate timing, the animals, birds and all such creatures on earth, sky and water, the beautiful plants, trees and creepers yielding edible and medicinal fruits, roots and leaves, adorning the earth surface and the necessary sunshine, seasonal rains and dew to foster all these to grow from the rich soil of the earth.

Creating woman to be the mate and peer of man and placing them in the Garden of Eden, turning them out from there because of their disobedience to God's commandment, their coming out to live in this world as man and woman and multiplying in this world of cares and troubles, make history as it goes on from generation to generation.

Man Created in the image of God

We human beings are very much different from other living beings on the earth. Because, man is created by God in His own image, wherein abides a soul of God's making. Though, according to physical biology, man is also a biped "animal" a soul in that body makes all the difference between man and other animals, domestic or wild. To evolve all the creatures other than man, God commanded "Let the earth produce all kinds of animal life; domestic and wild, large and small — and it was done. So God made them all" (Gen. 1: 24). But God created human beings making them to be like Himself (Gen. 1: 27) and He breathed His life-giving breath into his nostrils and man began to live (Gen. 2:7). Other creatures like monkeys having no soul in them, cannot become man by any evolutionary process by efflux of time. In the known history of thousands of years there is no such incident. The soul which is a creation of God cannot be formed by natural evolution from any other creatures, though there might be possibilities of metamorphic changes of physical modifications or bodily changes in the physical structure of creatures produced by the earth in accordance with God's command mentioned above (Gen. 1:24). Such changes are only physical adaptations necessitated by their living conditions, environments etc. and not beyond that level to possess the intrinsic virtues like soul and mind.

Among all the living creatures on the earth, only man has got a soul, the marvellous creation of God in him. (It is the soul (*ātman*), the divine spark that vitalizes the mind and intellect).* The other creatures have got only a quickening force of life in them. That is not the soul. It is only an animation, a living bio-force that prevails in nature to sustain life in their physical bodies for a short period of apparent life and in due course fades away and ceases, culminating in their death. Therefore, even though they have a mind of very limited calibre, in the absence of a soul-inspiring mind, there is no intellectual vision or its creative application in life. Only man, who is the crown of creation created by God with the soul abiding in him, makes such distinction in intellectual powers and creativity.

God's Purpose in Creating Man

Why is man created with so much of specialties and distinction? It is because God has in it a special purpose.

As told by the holy fathers who used to receive divine messages and visions from God, there were ten legions of angels in the presence of God: They were:

1) Nuhrone (Lucifer), 2. Srophe (Seraph), 3. Chrube (Cherub), 4. Mouthe (Throne), 5. Moravohse (Domination), 6. Shulthone (Virtue), 7. Hylavose (Power), 8. Reshenuvose (Principality), 9. Reeshmalakhe (Archangel), 10. Malakhe (Angel).

---

* *Kathopaniṣad*, p. 71 (English version by Swamy Chinmayananda).

Among these, the most eminent Legion, the Nuhrone (Lucifer), manifested a spirit of pride and was therefore cast out from the presence of God "down to Hell and delivered into chains of darkness to be reserved unto judgement" (II Peter 2: 4).

"And the angels which kept not their first estate, but left their habitation, He hath reserved in everlasting chains under darkness unto the judgement of the great day" (Jude Verse: 6). The evil spirits that have been cast out are known" as Lucifer, Beelzebub, Satan, devil, etc. In order to fill up the place from where this one legion of angels were cast out, God has created man in a much more glorious state than they, in His own image and resemblance.

Regarding the creation of man bestowed with free thinking ability of the mind, the prophet David says: ". . . You have made him inferior only to yourself; you crowned him with glory and honour" (Psalms 8:5). The hosts of angels were amazed to see God gladly watching Adam strolling in the Garden of Eden.

"God created Adam the man,
Exactly in His own image.
Wonderful creation strolling,
The avenues of Eden Garden.

And God so gladly watching
His creation of beauty perfect
Angels dumb with sweet surprise,
Marvel the rise of dust to glory."

"I will praise Thee; for I am fearfully and wonderfully made: Marvellous are Thy works: and my soul knoweth right well" (Psalms 139: 14).

In the body of man created by God so wonderfully for a very glorious purpose, dwells a soul, which is the creation of God and therefore the human body is the temple of God. "Know ye not that you are the temple of God and that the spirit of God dwelleth in you? If any man defiles the temple of God, him shall God destroy; for the temple of God is holy, which temple you are" (I Cor. 3:16-17).

God has given a life period to every one in this world as a good assignment of opportunity so that the soul in the human body, with its attendant free-willed mind may grow strong unto the perfection of Godly nature. When God decides that one's experience in life period is enough, the soul is called off from the body and that departure is called death. That is the death of the temporary body in which the soul was abiding till then. The physical temporal body becomes lifeless. The mind, which is the seat of intelligence, departs with the soul from the physical body. The temporal body from which the soul has departed becomes a lifeless corpse. There is no breath of life in it. Since the heart stops, circulation of blood in the body also stops. As the brain does not receive blood it stops functioning. When the mind and soul depart rendering the temporal body bereft of life and of any physical activity, decay sets in the body. In the ordinary course if the dead body is not interred within 24 hours, it rots and stinks so badly that it is impossible to keep it on the surface of the earth.

It is thousands of years since man has been on this earth. From where in the pre-historic ages this chain begins, is only surmise. However, a man's accomplishments are confined to a small period of time, till the curtain of death falls.

So Sure a Happening

Once born, man should die. It is sure. Therefore "Never forget there is death for me" is a philosophical note. It is very true; if one is always pondering upon death the various activities of life will become dull. However, it should not be a continual thought always to work through the mind. This note is just to keep a lingering consciousness in our mind that the life in this world is not a period to be spent in feeding and sleeping and whiling away the time, without any specific goal to attain. There is, however, a deeper meaning also in this and that is, primarily to maintain awareness about the real life beyond death in eternity. The entry into it is through the death of this temporal body. The aim of writing this book is actually to elucidate this fact.

Death, a Marvellous Phenomenon

Death is a marvellous phenomenon that approaches us through its own mysterious way at an appointed time. It inducts us into a completely different world in a novel but personally identifiable spiritual form. That form ensures that we are fully equipped with special gifts and graces obtained through Christ, making us thoroughly adaptable to the new environments of the spiritual world. As an inexorable law of nature, any living being should die. Therefore any person, however bold, will be helpless before death. Naturally, the fear of death is with every one.

The Fear of Death

Among the living beings, only man thinks about death and is afraid of it. It is because only he thinks deeply into the future intelligently. Still uncertain, it causes anxiety. Animals, birds, etc. do not have any such intelligent thought or visualization about the future and so they do not think about death and therefore have no cause for anxiety. If involved in any accident, excepting for the care of their own bodily safety and for means of escape, they are devoid of any thought about death. To get over the baseless fear about death, the only way is to know really what death is.

Fear of Death is the Guard of Life

Awful vigilance against death is a positive indication. None needs be ashamed of frightful thought about death. Because, fear of death is the guard of life, nevertheless, intelligently foreseeing the possibilities of hazardous situations and resorting to suitable means of safety are only precautionary steps. In an unexpected moment of the approach of death who would like to depart from the beloved kith and kin and friends and to set out alone on a journey of no return to a strange place? — Men are bewildered about what that place would be like and what is to be encountered there! What will man encounter after death and what would be the new experiences in future? Numerous such reflections are apt to strike fear into any brave mind. There is also a prayer even for deliverance from sudden death while yet unprepared.

The Death Pain

Great pain may be experienced due to serious injuries from deadly accidents or terminal diseases and other causes. When such bodily pain becomes unbearable there is the possibility of losing consciousness. Death happens when it becomes impossible for the body to hold on to life. The departure of the soul from the body by itself is not painful. Is anyone aware of or is in the know of how he was born or does he remember experience of any pain felt at that time? It is like that when we die also. While lying down to sleep, sometimes due to various reasons we may not get sleep though we long for it. But at an unpredictable moment we fall asleep. Dying is also like that. But the only difference is that the separation of the soul from the body will be known to the conscious mind later as the mind accompanies the departing soul. The mind realises that the soul has entered eternity. It is as if one who wakes up after sleep, realises the fact of his waking up. Following death, it is the waking up into a new life in eternity.

Death, a Necessity of Nature

That the human life period is limited to seventy or at the most eighty years (Ps. 90:10) by the creator, is in a good measure. Earlier it was about a thousand years (Gen. 5: 5, 8, 11, 14, 20, 27) and later limited to 120 years (Gen. 6:3). True there are some exceptions to this general rule. But if there is no stipulation of a short span of life, what would have been the condition on earth? The illustration of a Malayali poet Kunjan Nambiar in his poem "Kālanillatha Kālam" (Era Sans Death) is very uncomfortable reading. What a Hellish experience it would be to see grandfathers with their grandfathers and great grandfathers idling their time with pale and drooping countenance. The survival of previous generations remaining without death is unbearable on any count. Even though they might be physically fit, they would be mentally incapable of reconciling with the new ideological progress of the new generation and the problems due to generation gap would be multifarious. Therefore, their inability to reconcile with new progressive ideas and their ego of age-superiority with no fear of death, would make them most unbearable to the new generation. So it is necessary that the old generation should exit and give place to the new generation for the smooth running of the life-cycle and for all-round progress of the world.

Life Period — Only One Chance to Win the Reward

Further, if there is a certain period in view for the proper conduct of a life's responsibilities, it would be helpful to programme and be prepared to utilise that period prudently to lead a good and fruitful life. This sense of limitation of life period is also persuasive to ponder deeply into the reality that even while we live we are in the shadow of death and the active action time of this life is very short. We should remember that, in a sense, we are all actors who appear on the stage of this world for a specifically destined time to enact and complete our allotted part in the best manner in a short or long life until the curtain of death falls and we have to leave the lime-light for those who have to enact their role after us. It clearly means that *life in this world is a factual drama and not a rehearsal. While any mistake in the rehearsal can be corrected in the later performances, it is not possible in the actual drama. What is done is done. "What would be the use of immortality to a person who cannot use well a half an hour?"* — Ralph Waldo Emerson. Every person is born in this world for a specific purpose. That should be found out in devotion and lived fruitfully for the good of the world, and Glory of God to be continued in the Glorious Life After Death.

Not only man, but all the other living beings in this world also do come into being, live for a certain period and die. Again, new beings that spring up in the life-cycle by births and deaths, reveal the creator's boundless love and concern for the creation and its ever-fresh maintenance. If man co-operates with the laws ordained by God concerning natural provisions and environment required for our comfortable life, then even this world itself, according to the Will of God, will be Heaven-like. The exit of the old generation and ushering in of the new, as ordained by the creator in the natural course, is the divine programme for life conducive to its progress.

Earthly Life is Race to a Goal

If there is no end aimed at, there would not be a sense of attaining a goal in the race-track of life. Consequently one would not get the pleasurable experience of planning and joy of attaining success. Visualising a goal and seeing a path leading to it will help to attain the goal. St. Paul said: "I have fought a good fight, I have finished my course, I have kept the faith. Henceforth there is laid up for me a crown of righteousness, which the Lord, the righteous judge, shall give me at that day; and not to me only, but unto all them also that love his appearing" (II Timothy 4: 7-8). He said this with the satisfaction of having completed the mission that was allotted to fulfill in his short life. If one does not die at the appointed time when the human life period is run out, there would not be a sense of having reached the goal. And the most covetable goal reached through death, is the everlasting Glorious Life in Heaven enjoying the Sonship of God.

It is for that reason, when Adam and Eve when they ate the forbidden fruit of the tree of knowledge of what is good and evil and became sinners (Gen. 2:17 & 3:6) and yet though living in their mortal bodies, if allowed to eat the fruit of the tree of life also, may live for ever in that state in sinfulness, (Gen. 3:22) God cast them out of the Garden of Eden and put angels with flaming swords to guard the Garden of Eden. Otherwise the humans-turned-sinners multiplying in the same sinful body, without fear of death, would have been perpetually in a Hellish travail in this very world itself, devoid of any concern or sympathy for others and replete with envy and evil. With no reason for bereavement and with adding arrivals without departure, the earth would shape into an abode of anguish, agony and wretched suffering, a veritable Hell. To enlighten our thought about Heaven, there is nothing like death of relatives or friends.

The Greatest Benefit of Death

The anxiety caused by the very thought that our beloved ones may depart from us by death, will prompt us to express our love and utmost concern for them and to make them as happy as possible by rendering all loving services while they are yet alive. It is a prompting force that makes us always ready to render such services to all beloved ones, especially parents and nearest kith and kin. Further, the awareness that every moment that passes brings us nearer to death is thought-provoking pointer to the fact that we are all pilgrims in the world passing this way only once. In order to grow in peace and love, it behoves us to reconcile with things as they are and to forgive our foes and to love all our neighbours. Without fellowship with men there is no perfection and no Sonship with Heavenly Father to make our life-journey to Heaven reach its goal.

Suicide

Suicide is the utmost cursed act. Crimes against fellow men kill one's own conscience and faith in himself resulting in utter frustration. In ailing moments of acute agony, in desperate situations of biting spites, in the helpless struggle against miserable failures, in the lonely expanse of love-lorn feelings, unable to anchor on the love of God and men, one falls a prey to deep despair which wins over him to kill himself. Blind in thought and mad in action, man courts his own terrible end. Be it for any reason, no one should resort to this extreme step of ending one's own life. Suicide is a very bad act of deforming the sacred human life gifted by the loving Creator, and throwing it back into His very face. No other act is more expressive of utter hate and ingratitude. It is totally satanic. Sensing any inkling of anyone thinking in this way, one should dissuade him from it at the earliest as a brotherly duty.

Suicide is the culmination of an utter lack of love and faith in God. One fails to approach God who is the embodiment of love or to enter His realm of love. There is the possibility to fall into the thralldom of Satan. The life of some people, not motivated by love toward God and fellowmen, gets detracted from the path of love and righteousness, barren without charity, mercy, hope or faith in any one, or without self-examination, or readiness for long-suffering, culminates in suicide. With regard to a soul departing like this in committing suicide by force of circumstances, we cannot decide if his love and faith in God are totally lost or not, or whether it is possible for him to repent by self-examination after death and acquire the grace of remission of sins and purification of the soul. Only God, who knows fully well about that individual's real life and the circumstances that led to suicide and the mental set-up of the person at that moment, can judge whether the sin of suicide can be remitted in the Life After Death on merit of justification by faith.

To cite an instance, while establishing the Holy Qurbana, the Passover of the New Testament, in the Upper Room of Zion, it was Lord Jesus himself, fully aware of the intention of Judas Iscariot, who planned to betray him, speaks about that disciple: "Woe unto that man by whom the Son of Man is betrayed! Good were it for that man if he had never been born" (Mark 14:21 and Luke 22:22) and washes his feet, gives him the first Holy Qurbana and receives his kiss of betrayal at the Garden of Gethsemane, are matters worth pondering on. But after that, Judas repented about his sin saying: "I have betrayed the innocent blood" (Mat.27:4) and he cast down the 30 pieces of silver in the temple. A repented sinner, Judas, unable to bear the remorse, hanged himself to death. Whether Lord Jesus, who fully knows the circumstances in which Judas the repented sinner, unable to bear the compunction in his conscience, committed suicide, will accept the repentance of the soul of Judas and grant him the grace of justification by faith, is a divine secret of God's dispensation which is beyond our comprehension. We are nobody to think that God will never accept the repentance of the contrite soul of a man who has committed such a heinous crime. However we have the responsibility to avoid the circumstances leading to the sin of suicide and to lead a righteous life.

Euthanasia

Some people die without any apparent cause or symptoms and the person passes away silently as if nothing happened. But some others pass away after unbearable physical suffering or severe mental stress for a long period of time. Unable to witness the agony of some persons suffering excruciating pain due to terminal diseases we may perhaps tend even to pray for their death at the earliest to enter the eternal peace. In such circumstances some such sufferers may crave for mercy killing or may even resort to suicide. Then what is necessary is to confirm them in good faith in God and assure them of our ardent love. Apart from what happens when death occurs naturally at the appointed time, even if the patient or relatives request it, the Church does not approve of euthanasia, even though a few countries like Netherlands have legalized it. In the cruel punishment of crucifixion by Romans, before the victim's hands and feet are nailed to the wood of the cross, in order to reduce the excruciating pain, there was the custom of supplying strong wine mixed with a kind of potion that stupefies the brain. But when this was offered to Jesus, he purposely refused to drink it. The reason was that he did not want to reduce even a very little portion of the pain which he had to suffer in his physical body which he is offering as propitiation for the remission of the sins of the whole world or to cloud his mind in stupefaction while offering his soul into the hands of His Heavenly Father in the act of redemption of mankind.

But the use of anaesthetic agents in surgical operations and the like is a separate matter of medical treatment. They are not for comparison with the suffering at the end of life. But it is the perfect model that the faithful people should follow in the physical and mental suffering on the death bed as shown by Christ. It is our duty to pray for those who are called to suffer such tribulations for grant of necessary divine grace to suffer the pain in unfailing faith and hope in God and to console them by expressions of ardent love.

Of the two malefactors crucified along with Jesus, the one who repented also suffered the agony same as the other. Though both of them were on their crosses on either side of Christ at the same time and at the same distance from Christ, only one of them utilised the presence of Christ and his words. The agony he suffered led him to the means of grace through self-examination and repentance. But the other one passed away without making any use of the same opportunity.

Those faithful, for whom it may be the Will of God to be on the death bed with severe pain, should realise through the grace of the Holy Ghost that is the time given to them as the precious moments, leading to self-examination and repentance. They are moments for grant of the most coveted grace of entering Paradise to be with Christ.

We should remember and make use of the many exhortations of the prophets and apostles by conforming to the model shown by Christ.

How Job the just, in spite of passing through great sufferings and physical torments, without any fatigue, firmly holding on to the love of God, stood unfaltering, is a good example for us. We should understand God's divine love in purifying our souls by granting the grace of passing through the fire of severe physical sufferings, like gold smelted in a crucible for purification in fire. For some people, this sort of suffering might be for a long term by which the faith in God will grow stronger besides building up of strength to withstand the sufferings with fortitude.

About this, the Apostles of the Lord have given very many exhortations. In the early church how many martyrs have given up their lives in great torment. For them too, the writings of St. Paul have been of great inspiration. "For unto you it is given in the behalf of Christ, not only to believe on him, but also to suffer for his sake" (Phillipi. 1:29). "Who shall separate us from the love of Christ? Shall tribulation or distress or persecution or famine or nakedness or peril or sword? (Rom 8:35). "There hath no temptation taken you but such as is common to man; but God is faithful, who will not suffer you to be tempted above that ye are able; but will with the temptation also make a way to escape, that ye may be able to bear it" (I Cor. 10:13). "Forasmuch then as Christ hath suffered for us in the flesh, arm yourselves likewise with the same mind; for he that hath suffered in the flesh hath ceased from sin" (I Peter 4:1). "Wherein ye greatly rejoice, though now for a season, if need be, ye are in heaviness through manifold temptations; that the trial of your faith, being much more precious than that of gold that perisheth, though it be tried with fire, might be found unto praise and honour and glory at the appearing of Jesus Christ" (I Peter 1:6-7). "Blessed is the man that endureth temptation for when he is tried, he shall receive the crown of life, which the Lord hath promised to them that love him" (James 1:12). "It is good for me that I have been afflicted: that I might learn thy statutes" (Psal. 119:71). "Behold, for peace I had great bitterness" (Isaiah 38:17).

The Relief by Death

But by any means, when the curtain of death falls, everything is peaceful. When the sign of life is not there in the still body, one stage is over and life enters another stage. Death in the physical body of this perishable world is the beginning of the spiritual life in the unperishable world of eternity. Things happening in this world until then can possibly be seen and understood. But who knows about the spiritual experiences of those who pass beyond that? Nowhere in the Bible can we see the spiritual experience of any person who has passed over to that from the light of his own personal experience. Even though the Bible says that Jesus Christ has brought back to life three dead persons; daughter of Jairus (Mark 5:41), the son of the widow of Nain (Luk. 7:14-15) and Lazarus who was dead and interred for four days (John 11:39), there is no record of their telling their experience in the other world. Nor has any one enquired of them and gathered any particulars thereof.

A Witness Received About the Experience of the Other World

Our late Mar Yoohanon Mar Athanasios (Bethany) who had been declared by doctors attending on him clinically dead due to serious illness came back to life and lived for some time. During that period what His Grace had told one person as recorded by him in a biography (in Malayalam) on page 44 of the book "Minni Maranja Jyothis" (A light that Glittered and disappeared), is in the excerpt hereunder:

"His Grace, with a cheerful countenance was relaxing on the bed and talking to his own brother Babu. I kissed the Holy hand and stood nearby in reverence. In a happy mood His grace asked me "Have you ever gone to Heaven?" When I asked in reply "How is it possible," His grace explained to me like this: "I have seen Heaven and entered Heaven. Not today, when I had undergone operation at Vellore Hospital. Ha! What a beautiful house! Angels in the presence of the Lord were reciting Psalms unceasingly. Heaven where indescribable light radiates everywhere. Holy souls of radiant beauty welcomed me with overwhelming joy. I have experienced spiritual solace. By that time thousands of human friends were praying with warmth of heart to send me back to the earthly life. God the Father heard that prayer and sent me, this frail person back. I came to the hospital room and opened my eyes." Hearing this witness we adored that divine power again and again. His grace used to relate this incident to many till death."

But what his grace said to have seen Heaven in the spirit might be Paradise. Entry to Heaven is only after the resurrection of all the dead and including those who are alive at that time of Christ's second coming and the Final Judgement. About that there is explanation hereafter.

An Incident of a Dead Person Coming Back to Life

About 55 years back God granted to the author of this book, a very rare privilege to personally witness a very unusually miraculous incident. As I could immediately gather from the person involved in that incident very clear and utterly factual details thereof, clearly remembering even now, I am putting them on record hereunder, as they are relevant for discussion in this context:

One day I could observe a woman who died because of a disease by which she was continuously writhing with pain day and night. The still body indicated all signs of death. Very strangely, after some time she opened her eyes and began to talk and struggle with pain. Having understood that she came back from death to life, I tried to gather as much details as possible from her experience in the spiritual realm during the time her spirit was out of her body. She answered to all my questions. The facts thus gathered from this most uncommon incident regarding the great happiness provided for us by God in eternity were found to be perfectly corroborative with the facts stated in the Holy Bible. So it was possible for me since the last many years to explain these to many people, especially to those who were undergoing severe physical pain due to injuries in accidents and deadly terminal diseases and console them by the assurance of the eternal bliss that awaits them in the Life After Death. This helped them to visualise that solace ignoring the temporary physical agony and to be prepared for the happiness in eternity with self-examination, repentance, faith and good hope.

Therefore this book is written with the fervent hope that even after my lifetime this ministry will continue to render the benefits through this book to those sufferers who read it. Allaying the fears about death and assuring that it is the door which opens to great happiness that is provided for human souls in eternity, this book will help anyone to realise that the suffering here is only to prepare us to gladly seek the presence of the loving Saviour when he calls.

That most uncommon and marvellous incident was as follows:

One of my distant relatives, Mrs. Aleyamma, Mangalamadhathil House, near the Simhasana Church, Puthenangady, Kottayam (Kerala), aged 57 years, had an attack of a rare disease by which her entire body was swollen with excruciating pain. She was writhing with pain and wailing day and night. I used to visit her occasionally to console and pray for her relief. On one such occasion I saw her lying still. Only her mother aged 84 was there at that time. On seeing me she broke down and said "My son, she is dead — you please close her eyelids — my hand does not come for that." I, only 24 at that time, quite inexperienced in such things, stood hesitant. Yet as a check up I tried to feel her pulse, which was nil.

Silently two or three minutes passed and then her eye lids closed automatically and in the next moment opened in a lively manner as if opening into consciousness. Then she began to move her limbs as if struggling with pain and began to cry. Seeing me she enquired. "Son, why did they cast me back into this body? It would have been better if they had kept me there only." And she continued to wail.

By this I understood that her soul had left the body and she had gone some distance in the path of death leaving the sickened body, and after experiencing a little of the solace and happiness of the other world, her soul had come back to the same physically sick body.

In order to gather the details of the strange experience she had in the short stay in eternity, which nobody in this world ever tasted, I kept asking short questions and got very valuable information.

1. Were you not here? Where had you gone?

   She said: "Yes, I was not here, had been far far away. I was very happy there. No pain or discomfort. I am very sorry they put me back here in this aching body."

2. How did you go there?

   That was very simple. While I was lying here in great pain I felt great weakness in my body and the pain gradually reducing. I felt my bones getting loose. Darkness entered my eyes and I was in complete darkness. Then I sensed that I was getting out of this body and going into thick darkness. I felt as if I was in a different body moving fast into space and as if I was flying or shooting into darkness. While proceeding like that I could see far away a small speck of light. I felt as if that light was drawing me towards it, as it was becoming brighter as I went shooting forward."

Though she was expressing about terrible bodily pain in between, I was urging her to speak of all the details of her experience.

She continued: "When the light became brighter around me, there was no trace of darkness. Then I realised that I died and was taken away from the world of suffering. I continued flying like cotton in the wind in absolute weightlessness. Then I could hear good music and smell good fragrance. Looking around I could see angels."

3. "How were the angels in appearance?"

   "They were like good looking people, wearing white robes with flowers in their hands and very friendly, as if they knew me earlier. They were escorting me somewhere. I felt I was also wafted along with them effortlessly. Everybody's face was shining with expression of abundant love.

   "While proceeding like that I saw my departed father. He was in good form and with a shining face. Then I could see my son who left me in his infancy. He too was in good form. Both of them recognized me instantly and it was as if they were waiting for me. Oh what a joy it was to meet them.

4. "When you left this body did you leave all these clothes here? Then, when you were going with the angels how were you clad?

"Oh that is a good question" (While she said this, even on that pain-tinted countenance, there flashed the shine of a little smile)

"I felt that I too had the same kind of dress they were having. And I do not know when I got it or when I lost it. These rags were not there."

Still writhing with pain she was again asking me in anguish "Why did they put me back from that place of happiness to this body to undergo this suffering?"

Saying that it is the place to which all of us have to go, I consoled her and continued my enquiries.

5. "Then what all have you seen there?"

   "I felt that they were escorting me to the Lord. Though none appeared to move their lips, whatever anyone had in mind the others could understand. Therefore I understood that they were escorting me towards the Lord."

6. "Could you see the Lord?

   "Oh He was far far away, the great Light, much brighter than the noon sun, none can look at that brightness; could only imagine that God is there, but not possible to see or go near. But we were proceeding towards that light."

   "Then suddenly a loud voice sounded: "Not yet time." At the same moment they left me into this body."

So she was groaning and wailing. I consoled her saying that she had the exceptional good fortune just to pass over to the other world of eternity and to get a glimpse of the great happiness and joy that await us in the abode which God has provided for those who love Him. I told her: "let us pray with good faith to grant us the necessary fortitude to endure the suffering ordained by God until the soul is taken from the body, for purification of the soul as the grace-worthy experience to inherit eternal solace."

Arrangements were made to administer to her the Holy Sacrament of Unction on the next day itself. After receiving that the next day, she passed away that evening. I hope she did reach that great happiness which she had seen. I am fully convinced that this lady who was on her deathbed with agonizing pain had not said anything other than what she had actually seen and experienced. Nobody has got any idea as to the experience we are going to have after death. But I feel that such experiences as these, which we get only very rarely, are the opportunities granted by the Merciful God to give us some revelation about such matters.

2

After-Death Experiences

THE incident explained in the foregoing chapter left me thinking deeply about the subject. Even though this was an isolated case by itself, I have been enquiring about case histories in the records of hospitals regarding the experiences of persons who were declared clinically dead due to very severe diseases or fatal accidents and came back to life. So I procured the famous books "Life after Life" by Raymond A Moody Jr. M.D., with Foreword by Elizabeth Kubler Ross M.D. published in 1977 and "You Live after Death" by Harold Sherman published in 1986. While going through the various case histories in those episodes of treatments recorded by them and on verifying the experiences recorded therein, they were found to corroborate very well with those told by Aleyamma. This has encouraged me to relate these very beneficial facts to those who are in great suffering to console and encourage them to boldly face adversities with fortitude and hope in the great happiness quite certainly provided for us in eternity.

Since the observations in the above-mentioned books are quite reliable, and the experiences in the other world detailed in them agree with the Biblical truths, it is possible to arrive at certain clear facts on the subject. But the doctors have revealed only the anatomical and psychological aspects in a scientific manner based on their observations. These can be discussed in detail later. Before that, the various aspects of the incidents are explained in detail in the light of Biblical facts as follows:

Experiences of the Soul that Departs from the Physical body

As hinted in the foregoing chapter, when the soul of any person departs from the physical body, even while realizing that something unusual or uncontrollable is happening, the person loses consciousness. But for those having more strength of consciousness, it may take a little more time for losing consciousness. The soul breaks open the prison wall of the temporal body in which it was confined till then and becomes free to enter into the new experiences of the spiritual world. The soul goes off separated from the temporary body without any thought or anxiety about it, not knowing whereto. But the direction is guided by someone. "And it came to pass that the beggar died and was carried by the angels into Abraham's bosom" (Luk. 16:22). Lord Jesus says.

The Light of the World

Lord Jesus who declared that "I am the Light of the World" (John 8:12), dawns himself on human souls, which enter the spiritual realm. What Aleyamma said from her experience that the flight of the soul begins in darkness and is attracted towards a source of light is supporting evidence to this. The light shining in more and more fullness while nearing, that beaming love visualised as divine light is the destination of all the faithful departed souls. The source of that light is the Lord Himself. As evidenced from Aleyamma's words any soul that approaches the light would understand this fact.

Those who Come for Companionship in the Spiritual World

Those who arrive freshly in the spiritual world will not be

alone for a long time. Other spiritual beings approach for companionship. They may be Godly or satanic in accordance with the status of the worldly life of that soul. Further proceeding will be in their company. From Aleyamma's explanation of her experience this is clear (Luke 16:22).

The Shining Vestment of Righteousness One Gets After Death

The vestments of the soul are not made up of any material known to this world. No dressing that covers the dead body at the time of death or at the time of interment can enter the spiritual world. All those will perish on the earth itself. The linen clothes that were covering the body of the Lord at the time of interment were found laid aside in the sepulchre itself after the Resurrection (Luk. 24:12) & (John 20:5-7). But after Resurrection when he appeared to many, He was clad in glorious vestments. Every believer entering eternity will have vestments, which are glorious according to the righteousness in the life while in this world.

When the Lord was seen by the disciples on the mount of transfiguration (Matt. 17:2, Mark. 9:3, Luk. 9:29). His raiment of righteousness was shining exceedingly white and glittering as light, as impossible for any washerman on earth to whiten — vide the words of the disciples. The glory of the bright and radiant raiment of righteousness that is destined to be received by the human souls in the Life After Death is what is graciously granted by God who is mercifully pleased in the good virtues earned during their lifetime on this earth.

The Creator who has Bedecked Man in Vestments of Glory Even from the Beginning of Creation

The glorious apparel of Righteousness that adorned Adam & Eve, the perfect creation in the image of God, was forfeited by their falling into sin due to the violation of God's commandment. Consequently they realised that they were naked. Though they were questioned about the violation of the commandment, the merciful God made clothes out of animal skins and clothed them (Gen. 3:21).

Later on, while the Israelites who became free from the slavery in Egypt were proceeding to the promised land, when they walked the desert for forty years, their raiment waxed not old neither did their sandals wear out (Deut. 8:4 & 29:5). That God, while calling His children from the battlefield of this world's life of fight against sin and temptation to the freedom of the Life After Death in eternity, will deck them with raiments of righteousness of unfading lustre.

The Fabric of Love and the Fond Memories Continue Unaffected Even in the Life After Death

Even though the relationships in the temporal life in this world are broken by the physical death the bonds of love out live death. We have seen in the episode of Aleyamma that she had identified her father and child and enjoyed the re-establishment of the love bond in the spiritual world also.

Not only that, in the parable of the rich man and Lazarus, even while the rich man was undergoing torment in Hades, he identifies Lazarus sitting in the lap of Abraham (Luke 16:23, 24, 27, 28) and being anxious about his brothers in the world seeks the means to save them from getting into the same place of torment. If a person, who led such a Hell-deserving life in this world, has come under the sway of the bond of love in the spiritual world, how much more the souls of those who lived in this world with selfless and Godly love would be cherishing the loving memories and relationship. How beneficially this fact is revealed in the mutual intercessory prayers of the living and the departed souls, is discussed in detail in the portion about that later in this book (See Chapter 6).

Where Abide the Spirits of the Faithful Departed?

Answer to this can be seen in the Lord's Words and the writings of the apostles. "Today shall thou be with me in Paradise" (Luk. 23:43). That is what Jesus said to the repented malefactor who was crucified with him. There need not be any doubt that this saving promise is for all the true faithful. St. Paul has written in his epistle to Colossians: "For ye are dead, and your life is hid with Christ in God" (Col. 3.3). That is Paradise. This pertains to the souls of those who lived in the true faith and departed. The transit of others would be to Hades, the place of torment. More explanation in the context of dealing with the subject is given in Chapter 5, Para 3.

Modes of Communication in the Spiritual World

Though there are multi-billion spirits in the spiritual world it is possible to identify a wanted soul in a split second. Now in this world by the progress of Information Technology there are facilities of getting any information through instant messaging from anywhere on the globe. But quicker than that from the very vast spiritual world Aleyamma could immediately spot out her departed father and child from among the multi-billion spirits.

As we can understand from the parable of the rich man and Lazarus told by the Lord, the soul of the rich man from the torments of Hades identified Lazarus reposing happily in the bosom of Abraham (Luk. 16:23). He requested Abraham to send Lazarus so that he may dip the tip of his finger in water and cool his tongue, and Abraham replied that it is not possible for there is a great gulf between them (Luk. 16:24 & 26). This explains the above mentioned facility of communication in the spiritual world and is a fact confirmed by the parable told by the Lord.

Communication that does not Require Sound Wave, and no Audiometric Hearing

There is no atmosphere in the spiritual world as on the earth. There, no one lives by breathing air. Therefore there is no transmission of sound waves for verbal communication by movements of the lips or tongue. The action of generating sound waves in the medium of air by pronunciation of any language or hearing it by the vibration conveyed to the eardrum for understanding, is not there in the spiritual world. There, anything a soul thinks can be understood by any other at any distance as if from an open book close by as witnessed by Aleyamma in her experience in the company of the angels. This is the fact behind the ability of the human soul which can directly communicate in spirit with its creator and sustainer, God the supreme spirit, at any time. There is no "far and near" there. Therefore in the climax of the all-pervading transparency of the spiritual world it is impossible for any one to hide any secret or act in falsehood. Everywhere there is the beaming of absolute truth. That the conversation between the soul of the rich man and father Abraham could be easily understood by each other in spite of the great gulf between them, is proof to this fact that in the spiritual world all secrets would be revealed in the all-pervading transparency in communication.

The Holy Place of Utmost Transparency for Expectant Souls — The Luminous Abode of Mercy

For the reasons stated above, nothing is hidden in the spiritual world. Therefore in that shiny world there is place only for the most genuine goodness and absolute truth. There is no place or admission there for any evil or falsehood. This is the Paradise of life where the Church Expectant lives in solace of comfort till the second coming of the Lord and the day of Final Judgement. About this lofty abode of happiness the prophet David said: "Lord who shall abide in thy tabernacle? Who shall dwell in thy holy hill? He that walketh uprightly and worketh righteousness and speaketh the truth in the heart. He that back biteth not with his tongue, nor doth evil to his neighbour nor taketh up a reproach against his neighbour" (Psalms 15:1-3) and "Who shall ascend into the hill of the Lord? Or who shall stand in his holy place? He that hath clean hands and a pure heart; who hath not lifted up his soul unto vanity, nor sworn deceitfully" (Psal. 24:3, 4).

But living in the ordinary life, who could live a life so "perfect even as the Father in Heaven" (Matt. 5:48) and enter into eternity? Because of faith in Christ the time of mercy they get in Paradise, can be utilised for further purification and development of the soul. About this more clarification is provided hereafter under the heading "Worship of God and Intercessory Prayer by the Soul in the Life After Death" (Chapter 6 - (A), pp. 100-02).

However for those evil souls having no life of worship of God or communion with God, but addicted to evil deeds by satanic instigation and entering the Life After Death with silenced conscience and no self-examination or contrition, it is impossible to enter Paradise. It would be possible for them only to get away from the enlightening transparency that reveals all hidden facts and evils in their heart. They could only withdraw to the dark world of Hades that is justly deserved by them. It is clear from the parable told by the Lord that there they will suffer torments as the slaves of the master whom they served during their life in the world. They will not get permission to come back to this world to roam about, nay, even for a drop of water.

Perfect Solace Beyond All Sickness and Suffering

The future of those who led a truly virtuous life in this world, and called to the Life After Death, is very comfortable. For them death comes as a wonderful and comfortable experience by which they suddenly, in a moment, pass from a state of very miserable suffering to a state of eternal life of utmost joy and happiness. The physical ailments or mental trauma will not affect the true nature of the soul. No one will ever wish to come back from such a happy state to worldly life which can be seen from the witness of Aleyamma.

Every One's Destiny is Individually Cared for

The Christ who said "I am the Good Shepherd" (John 10:11) calls his own sheep by name and leads them out (John 10:3). From this we can be assured that each and every human soul is individually in his attention and cared for with specially time-bound programme for each life. In Aleyamma's experience the sound announcing "Not yet time" is a pointer to this kind of individual attention destined for her soul's purification and without receiving the grace from the Holy Unction according to her belief, her life chapter in this world would not have been completed. Before that when she was escorted to eternity, it might have been the pronouncement of the Divine Will that was heard in the announcement "Not time yet." Therefore it is the duty of every individual to sincerely strive and attain the goal of life successfully. In the case of each individual every detail of life's performance is noted with utmost attention. Reward according to performance is in the righteousness of God.

After Death no Human Soul would be Wandering about in this World

Even from very olden days there is a superstition circulated in fanciful fables relating to the souls of people who died without any time for preparation or by accident. They say that the souls of such people, not getting spiritual solace, wander about the premises of their death: some of these, with certain vengeance and some in a helpful attitude, giving clandestine suggestions in mysterious ways from the spiritual realm. The cooked up stories that some people skillfully fabricate according to their imagination and attractive presentation, gain cheap popularity very easily and sell like hot cakes. This is because of the mental satisfaction these ghost stories offer to satisfy the curiosity of the credulous masses that are apt to believe any absurdity in the novel but fake events presented as if exposing the great secrets from the para-psychological depths of the spiritual world. Since this type of story-telling exploiting the inherent human weakness is found even in world famous classics like Shakespearian dramas too, it can be understood that ghost stories had been of great attraction to people of all cultures at all times, whether learned or otherwise.

Even though there is similar specialty for stories connected with Satan, demon, devil, elf, Beelzebub etc. the stories relating to known people who died, have got more attraction. The reason is because those who have at least heard about the events of their lives, could connect with the trend of the fabricated stories as apparently credible as they are likely to think in their after-life, and further some such matters may possibly be serving some ulterior motives of some persons. Ghost stories, belonging to this branch of literature that have got such a dramatic impact in presentation potential by concocting plenty of false events serve as a highway to easily invoke misunderstanding in the minds of the common credulous populace. This is an activity of immense pleasure and profit for Satan who is the embodiment of falsehood. Even today this branch of literature is flourishing as the continuation of his victory march, as from the beginning of ages, in entering enticingly into the matters unknown to humans and misleading them. But the souls which enter eternity will be either in Paradise or in Hades until the Day of Last Judgement.

Misconceptions about the State of Departed Souls in the Spiritual World

Scientists who understood that after death the human souls go to another world, which is beyond the nature of this earthly world, began to study this supernatural phenomenon. Since the mind would be accompanying the soul leaving only the temporal body in this world, scientific researches began working at developing parapsychology as a novel scientific field, aiming at getting recognition for their findings. Work commenced on this branch of psychology under the stewardship of the British psychologist Prof. William Mc. Dowgall, at the Duke University in the year 1927.

In spite of many attempts to develop this as a branch of science it has not yet been successful. Because the fact is that the energy behind this type of phenomena is not physical but spiritual. From non-physical energy only non-physical functions will turn out. Therefore non-physical topics will not come under the hold of physical science. So, in order to handle such topics the modus operandi invented was to base the study on the mind of a medium. Accordingly some individuals were identified as having special abilities to receive occult messages from the spiritual world. So the old methods of communicating with spirits were revived and psychic researches progressed in the western countries. As the psychic messages thus received were from the hidden mysteries of the nether world they were predominantly subject to the distortive influence of the deceitful Satan. Further, such communications were also biased according to the medium's own idiosyncrasy. Unfortunately it so happened that the researchers failed to understand these factors.

It is possible to understand this only by virtue of glorious character and firmness in the true faith. The approach of Satan would be very much convincingly deceptive as to appear so true to Heavenly divinity as in visions and revelations, as if the souls of any of our departed good relatives or declared saints, or sometimes as Jesus Christ himself, to mislead the common man. Therefore the Church which has got spiritual vision and awareness of the dangers of anyone thinking deep into matters of spiritualism and getting entangled in any such activities does not allow any one to get involved in such matters of the spiritual realm.

Satanic Deceits in Parapsychology

Westerners being people who successfully conduct researches into any scientific subjects and expand the boundaries of scientific knowledge and provide leadership in evolving beneficial theories and practical methods thereof, having ventured to expand their sphere of research in demonstrating practical animation of some parapsychological phenomena, have gone astray from spiritual realities. Since it was understood that phenomena like ESP (Extra Sensory Perception) which is related to mysticism and telepathy (extra sensory messaging or communication by mutual understanding of minds), precognition (pre-knowledge as in predictive prophesies) and clairvoyance (ability to be aware of entities beyond ordinary senses), are workable with human minds, in order to prove by demonstration that these phenomena are workable on the same analogy with the minds that accompany the human souls after their departure from this world, the efforts taken by these researchers, though very elaborate, were all in vain.

Even earlier, in the past few centuries psychic researches were carried out by many eminent intellectuals like Arthur Ford, Father Tob, Prof. Marcus and Emmanuel Swedenborg, in these spheres. Their observations and the comments of those who cooperated with them, were only cheap reading materials fit only to rouse grotesque curiosity like ghost stories, because their deductions inferred through mediums from obscure and somber backgrounds were utter falsehood and great deceits of Satan and not real facts or scientific principles.

Satan is always alert and trying to easily enter into the minds of people who are devoted in spiritual pursuits. About Satan who is always roaming about looking for chances to dissuade humans by alluring them with false promises that may appear attractive and glorious to the human soul, the Bible says "Be sober, be vigilant; because your adversary the devil, as a roaring lion, walketh about, seeking whom he may devour" (I Peter 5:8).

Satan the Hypocrite Putting Up a False Drama through Departed Souls not Available for Prediction of Future

It is mostly those who are curious to know about future that fall into this kind of snare. This tendency has got antiquity reaching up to Old Testament days. That the witches are persons who receive messages from the spiritual world by extra sensory perception (ESP) through departed souls and their utterances will bring secret matters to light and therefore they have got prophetic importance regarding matters which are to happen in the future, are accepted even by some religions. But in the viewpoint of philosophers they are relegated as debased ideas. Witchcraft was taboo in the Mosaic Law. "Put to death any woman who practises witchcraft" (Exod. 22:18). Even the Israelite King Saul, who was afraid at the sight of the Philistine army and not getting any answer from God, was going in search of a witch. So Saul disguised himself, put on different clothes and after dark he went with two of his men to see the woman. "Consult the spirits for me and tell me what is going to happen" he said to her: "Call up the spirit of the man I name" (I Sam. 28:8).

It appeared to them as if "Samuel's spirit" had come on hearing the witch's call. She said: "I see an old man wearing a cloak coming up from the earth," because she was a medium. "Why have you disturbed me" as if "Samuel's spirit" asked, and in reply Saul told of the great trouble he was in. Then Saul was told "God has abandoned him and has become his enemy and next day he will die at the hands of the Philistines." The spirit said that Saul will die the next day at the hands of the Philistines (I Sam. 28:16, 19). And we see that it happened exactly like that (I Sam. 31:3-5).

Anyone reading the incident in the Holy Bible may possibly think that it was the spirit of Prophet Samuel that appeared there and answered to Saul's question in such a manner possible only for a prophet. It was only the hypocritical drama that is stated in the Bible as it happened. What was the source of the message so unequivocally received regarding the incident that was going to happen the next day? There is the appearance of the deceitful Satan.

Satan who Handles "Truth" (Genesis 3:4-5)

"That is a lie" the serpent hissed "You'll not die." God knows very well that the instant you eat it you will become like him for your eye will be opened — you will be able to distinguish good from the evil."

See verse 7: "Instantly the eyes of both were opened." Don't you see this was a true prophecy? Because their eyes were opened they knew that they were naked. When God came to visit them they had to run away and hide themselves. Don't you see the painful result of hypocritically presenting the half "Truth" here! Like this, pretending to be our well-wisher, Satan is the greatest deceiver hypocritically entering into many of our affairs.

Saul asked for an answer about his future, but in no way God answered (I Sam. 28:8). In the circumstances of not getting any answer from God, from where did Saul get the answer to his question? The after-events as they are revealed to Saul are detailed in the Bible so that God's children may think and understand the truth.

Satan who has got Mastery Over Branches of Parapsychology like Telepathy, Precognition, Clairvoyance etc.

Satan has got the ability to know in advance events that may happen in the future. If "Samuel" should know what is going to happen to Saul the next day, it should have been only from God. Though Saul asked God for revelation and God had not granted the request, how could the answer be granted by God through the spirit of "Samuel" by means of the witchcraft of a woman against God's own commandment? It can never be anticipated. That message was not from God. The spirit that appeared as a messenger was not the spirit of Samuel too. It was a hypocritical drama enacted by the lord of all witchcraft, Satan himself.

Hypocritically Acting as Human Soul

The witch, who acted as a medium to bring the soul of "Samuel" as desired by Saul, visualises an old man wearing a cloak and Saul mistakes the form of the old man as the "spirit of Samuel." "Samuel's" reaction: "Why have you disquieted to bring me up," is so naturally and spontaneously presented as a true dialogue by Satan himself! In giving a false impression that human soul is remaining in perfect tranquility, and in enquiring "Why I am disquieted," how much of naturalism is there! Why then Saul should suspect? The response is so apt to make believe that it is surely the spirit of "Samuel" that is answering through the medium. How credibly the impersonation is acted upon in the hypocritical drama! This sort of acting tactics of Satan the great deceiver is embarrassing many and successfully going on even today. "Well, no wonder! Even Satan can disguise himself to look like an angel of light" (II Cor. 11:14). Even many intellectuals have not understood that it is mere falsehood. Spirits of departed people will not appear at the call of wizards and communicate through them and it is really Satan who is behind all these hallucinations. Then what to tell about the common man's understanding?

Actual Experience of a Young Believer who Identified and Vanquished Satan who Came Hypocritically Acting as a Human Soul

An article written by the author of this book in the 2000 February/March issue of the bimonthly "Sathyaviswasa Deepthi" of the Kottayam Diocese of the Malankara Orthodox church, is excerpted hereunder as it is pertinent in this connection: — In 1945-50 period when Rev. Fr. K. Philipose (later Philipose Mar Theophilos) was the vicar of the Kottayam Cheriapally — A period when the Sunday school, St. Mary's league, Youth league etc. were very actively on service. After the classes the Sunday School teachers used to assemble in the Church for a special meeting of a Guild formed for special prayers, discussions about spiritual experiences of each, and about visiting poor and sick people in the locality and rendering them the necessary free medical aid etc. One among them was C.V. Mani Chakkalapparambil (Later Yoohanon Mar. Athanassius of Bethany) from which one could understand the moral and spiritual standard of the Guild members.

The Guild members, apart from the Sunday programmes, had some unwritten practices which had to be observed during the week days. Besides the disciplined life during the week, communion with God in the solitude of the night hours, self-examination, devotional prayers for the indwelling of the Holy Ghost, dedication for a renewed life etc. were observed. Whatever be the experience of each, it was discussed in the Guild meeting the next Sunday. Accordingly the spiritual experience in secret prayer, devotions and benefits thereby, were being very seriously discussed. This was very useful to all the Guild members for maintaining a spiritually unifying friendship besides gaining spiritual strength required for purity of character and a victorious life.

Some witnesses of those days were very memorable and one most specific among these, is quoted here-under as it is hoped that it would be beneficial for the faithful. This is the account of the personal experience of a Guild member. Since this is a matter of the soul's secret in the personal life of an individual, this is written with his concurrence on the express condition that the identity of the person will not be divulged to any one. He was narrating the very wonderful experience in life to the other Guild members:

There is a little background for this. As he had read some articles that appeared in the Malayala Manorama regarding*

Planchette, he thought that it was possible to communicate with the spiritual world through it. Further, he also felt that if one could concentrate well, messages can be received at the finger tip even without the medium of a Planchette. As it is possible to contact the limitlessly vast expanse of the spiritual realm by making use of such media there is the possibility of getting entangled in the deceitful snares of the deceiving Satan ultimately leading to spiritual hazards, the Church does not allow any contemplation or trials like this. Therefore more details of it are not described here. More so because this article is about the dangers unto which such attempts will lead to.

Though the said Guild Member reached up to the brink of danger because of his inquisitiveness, by the grace of God acquired through the merit of his character and devoted life, he could immediately realise the seriousness of the hazardous situation and could retreat from the path of deceit by Satan.

The Guild member described his experience as follows: "Woke up as usual one midnight and knelt down for communion with God. In a spirit of self-renunciation in the ecstasy of the soul that progressively develops by concentration of the mind, my body, mind and soul in unison were transcending towards the lofty divine region of celestial communion. In the ethereal happiness of the blessed moments for the grant of benedictions the creation of His handiwork was waiting in the secret garden of the soul.

Abruptly it happened. "Drop down your right hand and touch the floor with the index finger. I shall give you a

---

* (Planchette is a heart-shaped small board mounted on three multidirectional castors and a pencil with its tip coming down through a hole in the centre of the board, used by occultists as a medium for automatic writing and supposed as spirit-messages).

message." "A command flashed to mind from somewhere. Just like Samuel the boy, responded: "Speak Lord; for Thy servant heareth," (I Sam. 3:10), our Guild member also responded and waited. Having kneeled on the floor for prayer the tip of the finger was exactly touching the floor. Because of the knowledge about planchette it was thought that messages from the spiritual world can be received by this means.

The moment the fingertip touched the floor there was a wonderful experience. A feeling of numbness that started from the tip of the finger came up to the shoulder. Then as if some one had grasped completely, covering in the hold, the hand came under the control of someone. The finger devoid of any control of self, as if some one else was holding and moving, was continuously drawing circles on the floor. Then came a message in the mind: "I am a soul sent from the other world to tell you good things." As if in answer to the question "Which soul?" the hand wrote on the floor "Aleyamma" (In Malayalam language). In a previous meeting we had discussed as a subject, the special spiritual experience of Mangalamadhathil Aleyamma and her blessed death. Therefore the Guild member thought that God might have sent a good soul to give him some good message (It is about this Aleyamma's first death experience that is stated earlier in this book). The Guild member still on his knees, waited with amazement and happiness for the good messages that were about to be received through the 'good' soul sent by God. Then the finger was made to write on the floor in Malayalam figures ൫൭ (57) — Aleyamma's age at death, as if offering a proof. Obviously by this it means that it need not be doubted that it was the soul of Aleyamma herself that has come on the hand, because 50 years back from that date, the figures in use by all people in Malayalam territory and in Malayalam Schools were this type of old Malayalam figures. And therefore in Aleyamma's knowledge and so in her writing this Malayalam figures only will come, and not the modern Roman figures. Oh what a natural and believable writing! See what a great expert is Satan in the execution of his cunning plans!

As the means of spiritual communication had become clear, "Aleyamma" is asking: "Son, what help do you want? Anything you can ask." Our Guild member, aged about 25 years at that time, with a good job and fair provision of everything necessary for livelihood, did not have any pressing wants. But he had a hobby of participating in the crossword puzzle contest put up by the Illustrated Weekly of India at that time (First prize carrying Rs. 40,000/-). Therefore he asked whether it is possible to get the answer for the interlock words at the four corners. "They have not decided on the correct answer, let it be afterwards" the finger wrote.

If so nothing else is wanted he said in his mind.

But "Aleyamma" was not going to leave the dialogue at that. For sometime the finger was drawing circles on the floor. Suddenly a picture flashed in his mind. The figure of a girl in the neighborhood was presented in his mind. "If you like her. . . . ." It is unfair to write the rest of the message here. Immediately at this the Guild Member realised that it is not the soul of Aleyamma that had seized his hand but in that name it was the treacherous Satan himself. "Get out you cursed Satan" said the youth with great vehemence and in the same moment the numbness of the hand ebbed out as if water filled in a rubber tube flows out through a hole made at the bottom, and his hand was freed.

See how the cunning Satan tactfully approached to entice a youth who woke up at midnight and was kneeling in prayer, to dissuade and topple him. The youth knew very well that the soul of Aleyamma could never think in that way and immediately realised the deceit and vanquished the devil. Hearing all these details we were all wonderstruck."

From this incident we can understand one thing that after death, human souls will never come back to the earth and possess other living humans. Such fake stories are the hypocritical dramas of the neat cheat, Satan. True and faithful people will never fall into such deceits.

Departed Souls Get Separated in the Spiritual Realm

Taking advantage of the ignorance of people regarding the state of human souls after death, what all deceits are being perpetrated by Satan can be understood by the above incident. Immediately after death, the human souls do not go either to Hell or Heaven. The human souls which enter the spiritual realm can only go along with either angels or attendants of Satan according to spiritual status they have acquired, that is, according to their deeds while in the life in this world. Like this there will be a separation into two directions as undoubtedly said by Jesus Christ in his parable of the rich man and Lazarus. "And it came to pass, that the beggar died, and was carried by the angels into Abraham's bosom; the rich man also died; And was buried; and in Hades, where he was in great pain, he looked up and saw Abraham, far away, with Lazarus at his side" (Luk. 16:22, 23). These are the two places where the souls reach according to their spiritual status.

What is mentioned as the bosom of Abraham is the state of tranquility where the human souls who have reached the conclusion of their life in this world in the fullness of love and faith, continue to live in the same bond of relationship with God — where they wait in communion with God, receiving divine grace and peace in plenty, till the day of the Last Judgement. This is Paradise of joy and happiness. This is the very place of spiritual happiness for human souls in the loving accompaniment of God's angels where they worship God along with them and attain justification by faith by true and perfect contrition getting remission of sins and growing from holiness to holiness. But such people, who lead a life immersed in transient carnal pleasures, devoid of love or faith in God and fellow beings, living in utter selfishness like the rich man, will only be going the way leading to Hades, without getting admittance to Paradise.

However pure might be the life concluded in this world, it is impossible for any human being to reach the perfection of life like the Father in Heaven (Matt. 5:48). That is why, on death it is impossible for any one to inherit Heaven. Therefore, though the period of action is over by the conclusion of the worldly life, the loving and merciful God has provided for humans in the Life After Death, a period of mercy while waiting in Paradise to acquire remission of sins and to attain grace of justification by faith and to become eligible for admittance to Heaven,. Similarly, however wicked a person might be, without throwing His creation soon after death into Hell, it is the love of God that sends that soul to punishment in Hades. Punishment according to transgression is the justice of God. The torments may be great or less. There also is the opportunity for grant of grace by repentance and faith that invokes justification to attain Salvation. This is discussed in detail in Chapter 9 that categorically explains Hades and Paradise.

3

Experience of the Soul after Death
From the Witnesses of Reputed Doctors

THE case histories recorded by very famous doctors who could gather some facts directly from some very extraordinary experience in their medical career and explained in the light of their medical expertise in the books referred to in the previous chapters, are discussed hereunder, as they are relevant in this context.

Elizabeth Kubler Ross M.D., who wrote the Introduction to the book "Life After Life" by Dr. Moody, after reading the pre-publication copy has recorded that for the past two decades she had been deeply studying the state of affairs of those suffering agonizing terminal diseases, while dying, and the spiritual experiences of those who have come back to life, and that the facts she gathered have very much coincided with what is witnessed by Dr. Moody in his book. It is also recorded that all those who had undergone such wonderful experience, gave witness that on separation from their material bodies they felt as if rising up in the air and going about with great ease, and some helpful beings joining them as companions and seeing their earlier departed relatives coming to receive them.

Criticism from the Clergy

Elizabeth had forewarned Dr. Moody that, by the publication

of this book he would have to face severe criticism, especially from the clergy. She had also observed that the clergy in general have the opinion that this matter being prejudicially viewed to be in the area of mere superstition, it is better that no one tried to bring anything to light or discuss it. Even the very credible and clear account of the experience of Aleyamma, explained in the previous chapter, when I sent to a prominent church magazine, the Chief Editor, who has been my good friend, informed me that he does not propose to publish it, because such matters may create many problems. Then I could not but help to realise how truly the observation and warning of Elizabeth Kubler is seen fulfilled here also.

She observed that there will be members of the clergy who will be upset at any one who dares to do research in an area which is supposed to be taboo, and some religious representatives had already expressed their criticism on studies like this, and that the question of Life After Death should remain as an issue of blind faith, and should not be questioned by anyone. The clergy whom we believe are responsible for conveying to the people the remission of sins through means of Grace for joy of attaining Salvation, are themselves totally ignorant about the state of Life After Death, as written in the Holy Bible "Eye hath not seen nor ear heard, neither have entered into the heart of man, the things which God hath prepared for those who love Him" (I Cor. 2:9). Therefore the inquisitiveness to know about it, if stirred up, it would be impossible for the clergy to convincingly answer the questions of the common man, and in such circumstances the anxiety of losing their priority status in Biblical knowledge, might be the reason for discouraging any deep thinking in such matters.

Research into the Mysterious Spiritual World

Another hint was the response from scientists who regard

that the study into these subjects is unscientific. Though our present day scientific equipment are inadequate in this unknown area, Elizabeth boldly states from her own experience that corroborates with the findings in the investigations of Dr. Moody, that the true account of the findings in his researches will offer new points of view and useful information to anyone who comes forward with an open mind to enter into the secret boundaries of the spiritual realm. Therefore she concludes the Foreword to Dr. Moody's book expressing hope that those among scientists and clergy of good biblical knowledge, who are interested in research and bold enough to enter without fear into the unexplored regions of the spiritual world, may come forward, and try to find out the details and disseminate the facts thereof, not only for the information of those who desire to know them, but also for the people to believe.

What Happens in Death? — Informatory Witness from Reputed Doctors

Many facts about death have been described in previous chapters. We had a glimpse at certain matters of Life After Death based on the experiences of a lady who had passed through the gateway of death to the other world and came back to life on this earth in a very rare and uniquely wonderful way. But our knowledge about Life After Death will be very much enriched by understanding the true records in which world-famous doctors have explained what they have actually seen in cases where people who were declared clinically dead have come back to life. Some facts carefully studied and truly recorded from several such incidents as noted here are taken from the observations of doctors as well as the words of the persons concerned who have actually gone through the experience of death and come back to earthly life.

When the Soul Departs from the Body

A person nearing death feels extremely weak, while the body strength slowly sinks down. The conscious mind is subjected to certain special experiences. Bodily pains slowly reduce and the person may feel like hearing some strange and unclear voices in the darkness. Presently it is felt like as if one is proceeding very fast through a dark and long tube or tunnel, and a consciousness develops that the soul along with the mind is separated from the body. But still the person remains not far from the discarded body, along with the onlookers, and yet standing invisible to them. The departed person can see his discarded body lying still and all the people standing around it. But his existence cannot be seen by any one else. He can understand what they talk but it would not be possible to tell them anything or communicate anything to them by any means or respond to anything. It is an existence of a mere spectator standing apart quite invisible to all others and yet clearly viewing one's own body lying still and all the other things around. Before reconciling with that most unprecedented experience, the departed soul would be marvelling at the still-more new experiences of the spiritual world. What a freedom it is to quickly move about in space! What a thrill to fly up effortlessly diving down and speeding from one place to another, with ability to proceed to any place at mere will. However, there would be the consciousness of being in a body bearing a definite personality though not like the discarded body; it is an identical spiritual body.

New Experiences as a Spiritual Being

On separation from the body one could see far away a light the like of which has never been seen before. While the soul is approaching it, the darkness disappears by and by giving brightness everywhere. At that time he sees other spiritual beings approaching and offering any help needed. Upon seeing relatives and friends who have gone ahead he realizes to have reached the spiritual world; and in their comforting fellowship, all fears vanish. Their expressions of warm welcome are not by any words spoken by mouth or tongue but by thought emanating directly from their minds and exactly reflecting in the soul's mind. For that no language of this world is necessary. It is the language of the heart. Communication in the spiritual world is such that without any hindrance or impediment, things can be understood very quickly and perfectly from any distance. Therefore nothing can be hidden or concealed in the spiritual world. The mind will have a vibrant feeling of love, joy and peace experienced in the association of the new world. But at the same time all the incidents including one's own actions in the earthly life would appear very quickly and clearly in the mind. According to the transparency in the nature of the spiritual world all these would become already known to all the souls that come to help as well as to claim communion with the soul. It is in this situation the further course and experience of anyone will differ in the life eternal.

Though the experiences might be different for different persons later, there would be uniformity in general and fundamental matters at the start. Some people have said about their experience as if going though the darkness of a big tunnel, some others as going thorough a long and large cave, while some others as going through empty space and still others as going through a dark valley.

Special Experiences in the Spiritual Body

Like this, even if it is experienced as going far off in different ways at the time of the soul separating from the temporal physical body, some have said that they have been remaining near the discarded body, sometimes in an elevated position as a hydrogen-filled balloon, close to the ceiling, wondering at what happened to itself, not visible to any one but clearly understanding everything, and floating about in an existence lighter than that of cotton. To go out or get into a closed room, walls and closed doors are no bar, neither the roof for going up.

During this time of tranquility and freedom no agony of the disease or pain from any wounds of the accident that might have been the cause of death, would be felt. The reason is that the soul and mind together have come out of the body that was subjected to such suffering. Though one's own body might have been viewed in the dressing room mirror at a short distance, in this experience to see the body still more clearly in full dimension, is quite a wonderful experience as testified by many.

Witness About Very Novel Experiences

The transparent entity that has come out of the physical body in this way can be termed as spiritual being. A person, whose soul has been separated from the physical body for some time and has come back, witnesses that the spiritual being has not gone immediately anywhere else, but was nearby only. However, in its transparent condition at that time, it was completely invisible to humans. Even if the eyes of others turned towards the spiritual being, there was no indication on their faces for having seen it. Obviously, there was nothing in the spiritual being for them to see. So, for the same reason itself, even if the spiritual being passes through them, no one seems to have felt even as having touched them. The spiritual being does not have any material tongue, mouth or lungs to send air through, to make the vocal organs vibrate and produce audio waves in the air so that people can hear. For that reason the spiritual being does not produce any voice.

The soul has no need for that. It exists beyond matter, time and space.

Unexplainable Sensations

Because of the specialties of the spiritual being it is not subject to the earth's gravitational force. This is a state in which one can float about and move easily anywhere without the use of legs or feet. It is like what the disciples saw when they witnessed Christ "walking" over the sea. In this spiritual state of the being, it can go at a high velocity to any part of the globe or anywhere in outer space too. Beyond the three dimensions of length, breadth and height, this is a new existence in which other dimensions also would be experienced, as expressed by those who have returned from it to the life in this world. However, there is a record of the witness of a woman who came back to life, in which she states that while existing as spiritual being she felt as if her spiritual being was in the very same form as she was previously in her temporal physical body. She felt that it was possible to think more clearly and distinctly and to effortlessly understand very many things than she could in the physical body. There was no feeling of heat or cold, but feeling perfectly happy. There was no sensual feeling of the five senses of the physical body, of smell, touch etc. related to earthly substances. But the ability to see very far was beyond imagination. The power of understanding and capability to read exactly the thoughts of anyone far from view was quite wonderful. Mutual understanding of thoughts of others whether they are physical beings or spiritual beings, if they are thinking anything with the intention of communicating with others at the same instance, the soul can understand. Therefore in the spiritual world there is no need for a language for communication.

The Beautiful Spiritual Being, Though of High Transparency, is Incompatible for any Contact with the Physical World

If by any cause, a limb was mutilated or lost from the physical body, in the spiritual being it would be beautifully and perfectly joined to it. But there is no need for the leg to move about freely to any place or in any direction. The spiritual being would be wafting in the atmosphere or in empty space. Though very close, one feels as if he is in another world having no contact with this world. If explained in another way, it is as being in a strange existence like an unknown being from outer space coming and remaining amidst the humans yet completely invisible to them. It is a unique experience of existence as a spiritual being separated from the physical body.

Meeting Other Spirits

Dr. Moody has recorded in his book what many people who came back to life, have stated to have seen other beings who came to their help. They have stated that many of those beings were spirits of relatives and friends who had passed away from this world and they could quickly recognize them. Their appearance was consoling to those entering the experience of death. In certain cases, since their life in the world was destined to last longer, the departed relatives and friends exhorted them to re-enter the physical body and continue their earthly life.

Visions of Inestimable Knowledge

A doctor relates the witness of a lady who entered the state of death due to severe haemorrhage following delivery and happened to come back to life. She was talking about the marvellous sights that cannot be explained in words. She wished everybody were personally with her to enjoy those beautiful sights. She said she was pestered by the thought that she was alone to see all those wonderful sights, though she was aware that none would be able to go over there to accompany her. Impossible to talk to any one in that loneliness or even to touch anything, she felt very bad in the isolation of that strange place.

Spiritual Helpers and Friendly Suggestions

While in such an experience how other spiritual beings come for help, is quoted by Dr. Moody from the words of many persons. In the experience of one: "It is enough if a thought arises in the mind wanting to know anything, immediately a flash will come to the mind with the required information, as if getting the answer from someone nearby. Though being aware that many are nearby and remaining in anxiety as to what is going to happen to me, I heard a super-human order to go back to the earthly life, and I entered my own body as if sucked into it" as witnessed by Dr. Moody.

The Being of Light

"In thy light shall we see light" (Psal. 36:9). In the findings of Dr. Moody's researches it is recorded that many persons have stated that they have seen a light beaming from a distant point. This was an experience in which the light was seen very dimly at first as a small speck, gradually becoming larger and shining brighter illuminating all around. However, this pure white bright light that shines very brilliantly is neither harmful to the eye nor does it create difficulty in viewing anything in the vicinity. Those who had the experience of viewing this light say that their heart whispers within them that this is the captivating radiation which bestows the purest love of a supreme personality. Any explanation about it is incomplete. There are no words in human imagination to describe the heart-winning brilliance that proceeds from the super-gracious personality towards the individual who enters the spiritual realm. The ecstasy of flying towards that Heavenly light of love which irresistibly attracts the human soul is unique and celestial.

Consensus of Opinion Even in Sighting the Light

Another matter of surprise in this is that the details of the witness of different individuals, irrespective of whether they were of different religious faiths or belonging to different ethnic backgrounds, have in totality witnessed this experience in the same way. Only that in the details of the explanation of the divine personality, that is the origin of that divine radiation, their individual religious background, faith, training and culture are observed to have been slightly influenced.

Since the many people who had been studied by doctors were mostly Christians, they were concluding that it was Jesus Christ. In the opinion of a Jew and another woman it was an angel of light. In the experience of one of no religious faith that light was only some personality. At the same time a Christian differed from the opinion that it is Christ. But it should not be overlooked that in all these responses, the opinion formed was from a short-time experience that they had. They could not get an opportunity to closely commune with that source of radiation as they had with the spirits with whom they could associate rather closely. They did not get enough personal experience closely with that personality to form a clear and un-mistakable idea. But this all-revealing and deeply inquiring radiation of light permeating into the innermost sensitivities, apparently searching in deep inquisition has been witnessed by many as a radiation of unusual capability for in-depth scanning research into the consciousness.

Evaluation of the Merits Earned in Life

Are you prepared to die and enter into eternity? That is, whether there is anything outstandingly worthy to be shown out from the experience of your past life? Facing an enquiry like that is the experience of many, as understood from the revelations of their memories. When one's past life with all its details of performance quickly shines in the conscious mind that basks in the shining divine light, one would feel as if he is standing at the brink of the question as what to answer. The praiseworthy and noble answer required is about any glorious achievement in one's life.

But it is noteworthy and extremely heartening that this questioning is not like what a criminal in accusation faces. What fills the mind which is subjected to the enquiry is the endearing feeling that the personality in the light is nothing but love uttermost. As the sunlight which puts forth luminance and warmth, makes anything on which it falls also luminant and warm, so does the radiation of love help one to examine his life in detail. Therefore the task of offering a satisfactory answer will gladly be taken up by himself.

Like this the witnesses of many persons about their own experiences have been presented by Dr. Moody in his research book. In one such witness, a person who was a Christian has firmly stated the Light he had seen was Christ himself, quoting what Christ said "I am the light of the world" (John 8:12). He was confirming that what he has seen as the source of light while passing through the dark valley of death is Christ himself, the ocean of love, waiting for him in eternity.

Loving Embrace of the Glorious Personality

Another person stated that while being in the state of death due to severe sickness, he felt as if his spiritual being was separated from the physical body and then he could hear very sweet music and was directly exposed to the light as if the roof and walls of the room were not existing there. The light was of wonderful brightness and permeability. Though the light was very bright, it did not dazzle the eye or interfere with the vision. It was such a pure light offering wonderful vision that cannot be compared to anything in this world. Though it was not possible to closely view the power of this divine light which is the radiation of perfect love and understanding, the existence of the supreme personality who is the origin of that holy radiation was undoubtedly worthy of belief. He continued: "its thought-provoking divine touch of love came upon me as a captivating question "Do you love me?" Admittedly it is wonderful that the waves of the extra-sensory impression of that radiation, which lovingly descended upon me as an affectionate caressing, made me to deeply realise the invoking of the message "If you love me, go back to the world and complete the life that you have begun." The witness concluded: "All this time the thrilling divine love and heart-winning mercy were fondling and thrilling me."

The Embodiment of Love which Extends the Earthly Life for Services of Love

Still another person says, "When that happened I was out of my physical body. I could see from above my operated body on the operation table. At this stage first I experienced much uneasiness. But soon a very bright light came. First it was a little dim. Then gradually gaining brightness it became a big gathering of light rays and was shining brighter than the sun. Though the radiation of the very pure light was extremely powerful it was not hurting to the eyes. Everything around could be seen clearly. The light as a personality was asking me "are you prepared to die?" The person asking is not visible. The question gave me the impression that it was put with the full knowledge that I am not prepared. Along with that I heard a message loudly in my mind that the axiom of taking to eternity through death or returning to the worldly life will depend on the concerned individual's outlook on life, earnest longing for the glory of God, concern for services of love, etc. Therefore thoughts conducive to self-examination rose up in the mind. Still the above-mentioned question was going down to the core of my mind. Besides, the light was conversing with me spiritually and I became deeply convinced that I am being loved to the uttermost and becoming completely recovered from the wounds of the accident. The divine love that permitted me to fruitfully continue in the physical life is beyond imagination and explanations."

Individual Witness Educative

The witness cited above will certainly be helpful to anyone to get a fore-knowledge about what would be the experience of an individual while entering eternity through death. Dr. Moody has well studied and recorded many incidents like these witnessing the experiences of different people. Because all these corroborate very well with the matters noted in the incident that I had the privilege to personally observe 55 years back, in which a woman had gone through death and come back to the world just for one day and to personally talk to her, I tried to study more about these matters requiring minute perception, and record many useful details, for the benefit of others.

4

Experiences of Coming Back to Earthly Life

From the Witnesses of Eminent Doctors

FROM the facts collected and recorded by Dr. Moody from the persons who have passed over to the Life After Death and come back to life, it is understood from their recollections that the reasons for their return were diverse.

Grace Granted on True Earnest Living

One decisive factor among the diverse reasons is the condition of the body discarded by the soul. If that body is diseased or bruised to such an extent that it is impossible to sustain life in it, there is no possibility of the soul coming back to it. In the case of Aleyamma I could observe that her physical condition was very bad. However it might have had the capability to hold on life for another day. Otherwise, having entered eternity, the soul that returned might have come back to the body imbibed with sufficient grace to sustain life in it for one more day. That, I believe, is God's dispensation of His Holy Will to allow her one more day of earthly life to enable her to receive the Sacrament of Holy Unction which she earnestly longed for to receive for more purification of the soul.

God's Grace that Grants Opportunities

Any human being getting an extension of life in this world is solely on the kind dispensation of God. He knows the innermost secrets of everyone's heart. He can understand the divine love-prompted dedication of every individual for utilizing God-given talents for the good of the world and Glory of God, and decides on granting the opportunity for that simply as a gift of His grace. Dr. Moody has recorded several such witnesses of persons who have received God's grace like that and come back to life for duties yet to be fulfilled.

The reactions of persons who have thus come back to earthly life have been different. For Aleyamma, because her body was in extremely diseased condition she was not willing to come back from the happiness of the Life After Death that she has tasted a little, as evident from her words. However, having received the Sacrament of the Holy Unction for remission of sins, though physically suffered for one day more, without any regrets she might have had the joy of entering eternal life with added grace of remission of sins and soul purification.

Mysterious Dispensation of God

The souls that have departed from physical bodies, rendered incapable of sustaining life due to excessive haemorrhage following delivery or deadly injuries from major accidents, may not be willing to come back from the happiness and joy of Life After Death. But in the experience of some whose bodies have been reconditioned suitably for sustaining life by modern medical treatments, they have been observed to have wonderfully fulfilled God's Will in carrying out their duties in this world after coming back to life.

For Duties Yet to be Fulfilled

After imbibing the mind-capturing ecstasy of the perfect love that the soul beholds in the light that is seen after death, there will not be any inclination to return to the earthly life. See how Peter, James and John, after beholding the wonderful celestial scenes of the mount of transfiguration and attracted by the Heavenly glory of the divine light, desired to continue there only (Mat. 17:4, Mark 9:5 & Luk 9:33). Still that love which is the origin of the light itself, is constraining them to return as revealed from the witnesses of some. Just like a father calling his son and asking him "Son, go and work today in my vineyard" (Mat. 21:28), this kind of sending back happens as an answer to the heart-felt prayers of the deceased's children and dependents as wonderful happenings described by Dr. Moody in his book.

Ennobled Living in the Resuscitated Life

Those who witnessed the above incidents as their own experiences had neither been suffering from any mental ailments nor were they any dream-tellers. They all were people of good sobriety and mental strength. Dr. Moody affirms that they have related the spiritual experiences they had, truly and sincerely, exactly in the same way that they happened. In the experience of some people, due to unbearable pain because of serious diseased conditions or very severe bodily injuries, the soul may get out of the physical body. In some cases those who have come back to earthly life, with a vision for leading an ennobled life have been observed to be very much involved in a service-oriented life, rendering very useful services to others and spending their after-life with a dedicated earnestness. One among them said that it is possible to see that earthly life is a period of utmost valuable opportunities. Even the very incomplete knowledge about the very covetable things provided for us in the Heavenly abode as seen and experienced by some would be prompting us to acquire as much graces as possible during the earthly life to inherit that unexplainably glorious goal. One would understand that there is a new meaning for life, and begets sufficient purity of heartened wisdom necessary to cultivate loving friendship with any type of people. Those who have thus come back show maturity of mind capable of understanding the needs and problems of others, as if living itself is devoted to extend the hand-touch of love to fellow beings. It is hoped that those who read this book also would show such a quality of mind.

Dedicated Life with no Fear of Death

However, Dr. Moody has witnessed that none of those who have thus come back to earthly life have ever thought that they are purified or blameless people, as could be made out from the talk with them. Irrespective of age, these people are interested in acquiring knowledge, as they have understood that it is appropriate and necessary to have it as an acquired wealth to life eternal. These people, who believe that they have to fulfill further duties of loving service in this world, unhesitatingly say that they are not afraid of death. It is not only because they have once passed through death, but also because they have seen God's love that outlives death and have enjoyed at least a glimpse of it in its splendor of luminance. Moreover, the assurance that there is a special will and plan of God for each individual and the hope that there is a warm welcome for each one provided in eternity, not only makes death void of fear, but as an incident full of hope. Therefore it gives one deep faith to get ready to go back there again. It is this preparedness that is most important, making life really fruitful. The consciousness that this coming back to earthly life, having received the loving mandate from the divine personality who is the light of light, and the readiness for performance and dedication to the purpose, makes the rest of the life worthy and positive.

State of Happiness After Death

A person who has understood at least a little about the Life After Death said: "About persons who say "There is nothing after death," we cannot but sympathise about their ignorance. We could only try to bring them to the hope of everlasting life in eternity. If we can believe the details of such actual experiences and when we participate in the funeral services, we should feel only satisfaction about the happiness into which they entered, we won't feel sad." *"While we are mourning the loss of one friend, others are rejoicing to meet him behind the veil"* (John Taylor).

Re-establishment of Love Bonds in Eternity

A woman says that she has felt as if she had gone to her own house and it was possible to see there her relatives and friends and enjoy their company again. Another person says: "To pass from the earthly life to eternal life is like getting promoted from one class to a higher class. Death is not the appropriate word for that. That is why we know them as "The Departed. It does not have the perishability of death in it" (It is like changing from the khaki uniform of the High school to the fanciful dress of the College). The special abilities in the knowledge and wisdom and talents of the soul, are as written: "What we see now is like a dim image in a mirror, then we shall see face to face" (1 Cor. 13:12). It is sure that more will be known only after we enter eternal life. In support of this, many doctors have got to say many marvellous experiences. Some patients, who had no knowledge of medical science after they came back to life, have stated in detail, all the steps that the doctors had taken to resuscitate them. This indicates that the understanding capacity of the soul is quite extraordinary.

Marvellous is the Understanding Capacity of the Soul

When the doctor said that he had to take great effort to resuscitate a girl, she said: "Yes I knew it!" The doctor thought at first that she might be just saying pleasantry. Then the doctor was stunned with surprise when she continued to relate all details of the treatments given to her from the time her breathing stopped, up to the time of seeing the signs of life again, as an eye-witness commentary of a medical expert. She added too, that it was possible to see all these in such detail because her soul was out of the physical body at that time. Dr. Moody has recorded that, to all the details asked by the doctor she answered clearly and easily without any mistake.

The light seen at the time of death signifies that the soul is passing to infinity. But the incidents of coming back to the physical body and then continuing the earthly life, are extremely rare and wonderful phenomena. Jesus Christ, while in this world, resurrected the daughter of Jairus, the son of the widow of Naine and Lazarus of Bethany, because the same kind of Will of God and mercy were bestowed upon them.

Soul Called Back to the Body to Continue Life in this World

In the above three instances recorded in the Bible the persons concerned were actually dead. It is definitely stated in the case of the daughter of Jairus that "Jesus took her by the hand and called out "Get up, child." Her life returned" (Luk 8:54). Further, when Jesus answered the messengers of John the Baptist who asked Jesus whether he is the Messiah who is going to come, Jesus answered the messengers "Go back and tell John what you have seen. . . . The dead are raised to life" (Luk 7:22). Here Jesus confirms that those people resurrected by him were actually dead. (To understand what Jesus spoke of death as sleep please read John 11:11-13).

Therefore we can be sure that there is the possibility of the soul going out of the body and according to divine dispensation, the soul may come back to the body to continue life on this earth till God's appointed time.

Scientific Case of Existence of Human Soul

The scientific world which was sceptical about the existence of human soul is now on a rethink about it. They have much knowledge about body anatomy and mental sciences. Engrossed with the phenomenon of Out of the Body Existence and coming back to the body to continue life, they are now at cross roads of whether there is an entity that lives after physical death of a human body — whether there is a human soul which is the real life in the body. In October 2003 issue of the Reader's Digest, Anita Bartholomew narrates an instance in which a Neurosurgeon Robert Spetzler and a British researcher Susan Blackmore PhD. spoke about strange symptoms observed in a patient Pam Reynolds, 35 years, who had undergone a brain operation in 1991. Under deep anaesthesia the entire blood in her body was drained off to a heart machine stopping her heart function and transferring breathing also to another machine. The brain surgery was performed for one hour after opening the skull with an electric saw. During that time life actually left her body and she was clinically dead. She met all the criteria for death.

Later when she was resuscitated she spoke about her experience during the time when her body was in a dead condition. She said that she found herself travelling through a tunnel towards a light. At the end she saw her long-dead grandmother. Then her uncle who led her back to her body instructed her to return. On returning she felt like plunging into a pool of ice water. On coming back to life she told the doctor all that she had seen and experienced. The doctor is still bewildered at this strange phenomenon.

According to the indication of different instruments, the doctor is sure that during the time of the operation there was no life in the body. He compares the body with a computer with no power connection. Absolutely dead! In this state what had been her experience? She saw the doctors working on her and her body as if she saw it from a distance, lying still. When the eyes of the body are closed and brain dead, who is that animate personality viewing at a distance and remembering full details for recollection on resuscitation?

People may see uncommon sights in a coma or in hallucination. But, for that the brain should function. In this case it is ruled out. This means life which requires all these vital organs functioning, has gone out of the body. That life is not in the hold of any doctor or psychiatrist. It has its own way of function and expression as revealed by this woman who had undergone such a very special brain surgery and revived.

Near Death Experience (NDE) and Out of Body Experience (OBE)

In this case the condition of death came into the body in the process of blood being entirely drained off to the machine to take care of it. So also the body stopped breathing as it was taken over by another machine. Eventually the brain stopped functioning; the body came into a state of clinical death. At this stage there is no chance for hallucination because the brain function is completely skipped. It cannot hallucinate. There is nothing in the body as mind or memory or thought. It is in a completely dead condition. The life is out. When the lower brain or brainstem which controls the automatic body functions stops working; it is a state of brain death. It is complicating for a medical professional to confirm whether this is a condition in which the person can be declared legally dead and is about to become an organ donor and is legally active or not. This is more poignant when the body can be kept functioning for long periods with life supporting systems and also, it might be possible to be resuscitated with CPR or other means depending on causes and conditions under which the vital organs had stopped functioning.

Now, when vital body functions are re-established and life comes back, the question remains; where did the life exist? The only explanation is, it is the human soul that has life and a mind with it. The soul, which is having life and mind, is able to perceive, understand and memorise many things much deeper and sharper as evidenced by the witnesses given by these persons who experienced OBE and returned to life. That is the evidence for human soul which may leave the body and may re-enter the body with memories of OBE to speak about the time when the soul comes back into the body.

There is Something that Lives After We Die

All people who had an experience of NDE or OBE have clearly given their experience of the phenomenon when they came back to conscious life in the body. This is stated by medical experts who attended on such people even in recent years. A study by British researchers, published in the journal of Resuscitation, found that in 11 percent of the NDE cases they had memory recall of the unconscious period. This indicates that consciousness could exist in the absence of a functioning brain. Life is out when soul is out and resuscitates when the soul re-enters the body, from where it was while in OBE. What survives death of the physical body is the soul with the mind to continue living in eternity.

A Serious Subject for Re-thinking by Medical Experts

Even now the medical doctors believe and argue that the experience of people who had Out of Body Experience or Near Death Experience, what they say in recollection, are only stories of hallucinative sights and visions they see in delirium of severe pain or intoxication. They are not inclined to believe that there is a soul which has life that may stay away from the body, under special circumstances described in previous paragraphs, though the persons who return to life very clearly recollect their experience in the spiritual world. The witness of Neurosurgeon Robert Spetzler would be an eye-opener to the truth of this strange phenomenon of NDE and OBE. Here opens the fascinating horizon of the Life After Death.

5

Hints in the Holy Bible About the Life After Death

> *"As the hart panteth after the water brooks, so panteth my soul after thee, O God. My soul thirsteth for God, for the living God. When shall I come and appear before God"* (Psal. 42:1, 2). *"I am God, even thy God"* (Psal. 50:7) — *"O God thou art my God: early will I seek thee: my soul thirsteth for thee, my flesh longeth for thee in a dry thirsty land where no water is:"* (Psal. 63:1).

Among many things stated in the Holy Bible about the human soul, there are many authentic and clear references regarding the Life After Death also. If the Bible does not deal with the experience of the human soul after death, what superiority has it over other books? Though these facts can be understood by those who read the Bible regularly and continually, the texts concerning Life After Death mentioned in different portions, if brought together in one book, would, it is hoped, be useful for sustained study and faith.

A Promise in the Bible About the Life After Death

The most important and hopeful promise that is given by our Lord and Saviour Jesus Christ is: "In my Father's house are many mansions; if it were not so, I would have told you. I go to prepare a place for you. And if I go and prepare a place for you I will come again and receive you unto myself; that where I am there ye may be also" (John 14:2, 3). What a great promise in which shines such a divine love! The Father's house is a permanent house, Heavenly and spiritual. The eternal house of happiness! Where he goes ahead of us and prepares for us a place to live with him in the Life After Death. We can believe it is a sure promise. This promise regarding the mansions prepared in the Father's house for humans who pass over to eternity, through death, confirms what Christ said: "And whosoever liveth and believeth in me, shall never die. Believest thou this": (John 11:26). But, however, to reach there, one should have the spiritual attainment of righteousness and freedom from sin. To guide us in our life in this world he has promised to send the Holy Spirit when he goes back to the Father who has sent him (John 16:5): "Nevertheless I tell you the truth: It is expedient for you that I go away: for if I go not away, the Comforter will not come unto you; but if I depart I will send him unto you. And when he is come, he will reprove the world of sin, and of righteousness and of judgement" (John 16:7, 8). Therefore we should always pray for guidance of the Holy Spirit and strive to live a life based on love and righteousness to deserve a place in the Heavenly Father's house in eternity.

More about this is dealt with in the Chapter "Last Judgement."

"Lord, who shall abide in thy tabernacle? Who shall dwell in thy Holy Hill?. . ." (Read Psalm 15).

Father's house is prepared for whom and how, are explained in the 1st epistle to Corinthians as follows: "But as it is written Eye hath not seen, nor ear heard, neither have entered into the heart of man, the things which God hath prepared for them that love him (I Cor: 2:9). However, if we examine the parables our Lord Jesus has told during his life in this world, we can easily understand the revealing facts about the Life After Death.

First let us learn what the Lord said about an individual who has departed form this world's life to eternity. What he said about Lazarus who died and was interred for four days? "Saying that "Our friend Lazarus sleepeth (John 11:11). Though many people said that the daughter of Jairus is dead, the Lord said: "Weep not she is not dead, but sleepeth" (Luk. 8:52). In these instances, by saying "Sleepeth" He reminds us that though the earthly body is lifeless the soul is very much alive. The only difference is that the soul which was living in the temporal body during the life period in this world, has discarded that and entered eternity. Then the temporal body becomes lifeless, but the real person continues to live in the spiritual world. Then the body is in a state of sound sleep from which none can rouse it.

But the manner in which a soul with a free-willed mind enroute to eternity lived in this world, will be a very decisive factor "For we must all appear before the judgement seat of Christ that every one may receive the things done in his body according to that he hath done, whether it be good or bad" (II Cor. 5:10). For more details in this connection please read Chapter 6 — p. 106 and Chapter 9 — pp. 169-70.

Danger Signals in the Life After Death

Every day several thousands of people are taken to eternity at the conclusion of their life in this world. But being cast into Hell is a peril that may happen in the Life After Death and one should try the utmost to avoid it. There are many danger warnings about it in the Gospels.

(i) Matthew: 5:29, 30.

"And if thy right eye offends thee, pluck it out and cast it from thee; for it is profitable for thee, that one of thy members should perish and not that thy whole body should be cast into Hell. And if thy right hand offends thee, cut it off and cast it from thee for it is profitable for thee that one of thy members should perish and not that thy whole body should be cast into Hell."

(ii) Mark 9:43-49

"And if thy hand offends thee, cut it off: it is better for thee to enter into life maimed, than having two hands to go into Hell, into the fire that never shall be quenched;

Where their worm dieth not and the fire is not quenched.

And if thy foot offends thee, cut it off: it is better for thee to enter halt into life than having two feet to be cast into Hell, into the fire that never shall be quenched:

Where their worm dieth not and the fire is not quenched.

And if thine eye offends thee, pluck it out: it is better for thee to enter into the kingdom of God with one eye, than having two eyes to be cast into Hell fire:

Where their worm dieth not and the fire is not quenched.

For every one shall be salted with fire and every sacrifice shall be salted with salt."

Since what is stated above is told by Jesus Christ himself, it has to be understood that in order to inherit the blessing of the Life After Death, any sacrifice suffered in this world will not be too much.

To enter into the kingdom of God as maimed or with one eye, should be understood in the meaning as clarified in the Gospel according to St. Mathew "For thee that one of thy members should perish, and not that thy whole body should be cast into Hell." That is, in the earthly life if eye or any limb becomes the cause to sin it is better to eliminate it and inherit

Heaven. It is only the earthly body which was maimed that would perish and turn mud to mud at death. *The body which will resurrect as glorified body into the Life After Death by bearing the image of Heavenly* (I Cor 15:49), *would not be having any lameness but be endowed with excellence and would be worthy of inheriting the kingdom of God.* In any case, as mentioned in chapter 7, as said by the prophet Ezekiel at the great event of the Resurrection of the Dead, ". . . a shaking and bones come together bone to his bone." *This means, on resurrection, any bone severed and buried earlier would be joined with the body which lost it.* Even though this is said about the organs of the physical body, it is meaningful in respect of other talents of life like different achievements, positions, authorities, abilities etc.

Where would be the Soul of the Faithful in the Life After Death? What would be their experiences?

When Jesus Christ was rejected and was crucified, a malefactor who was crucified alongside with him, while about to die, saw life in the death of the Lord on the cross, glory in disgrace, honour in shame, victory in defeat, kingliness in slavery by the spiritual eyes and prayed with repentance and faith to remember him also when Christ comes in the glory of his kingdom. Immediately the Lord answered to his prayer: "Verily I say unto thee today shalt thou be with me in Paradise" (Luk. 23:43). No more evidence is required to know where would be the souls of those who die after repenting over their sins and becoming worthy of remission of sins. But there is no hint about where goes the soul of the unrepented malefactor. About that we shall discuss later.

We are born of temporal body in this life. "God forbid. How shall we that are dead to sin, live any longer therein" (Rom. 6:2). "When we were baptised into union with Christ Jesus we were baptised into union with his death" (Rom 6:3).

"By our Baptism then, we were buried with Him and shared his death in order that, just as Christ was raised from death by the glorious power of the Father, so also we might live a new life" (Rom. 6:4). Therefore in the Life After Death which continues in eternity, we become worthy of happiness as said in the epistle to Colossians 3:3. "For ye are dead and your life is hid with Christ in God." This state of spiritual happiness is of utmost blessed existence because of sharing and growing in the abundant spiritual life of Christ. More details in this connection are given later here under the caption "Development of Spiritual life experience in the spiritual worship in Paradise" (Chapter 6).

Christ's Entry into Hades

Now we should know about Hades — what it is and where it exists. As explained later in this book in greater details under chapter 9, "Heaven, Hell, Paradise and Hades," Hades is a metaphysical entity not coming under the ambit of physical reckoning of man who lives in physical body in this physical world. It is totally a spiritual existence of the soul in the world of the dead, suitable to its intrinsic virtues. Adam and Eve, who were banished from the Paradise of Eden for transgressing God's commandment, had to be in Hades with their descendants under the captivity of Satan. To save them from there and to restore them to Paradise, the Messiah took the load of all the sins of the world on himself and died on the cross and expiated the curse of sin from the world. The resurrected Christ entered in spirit into the world of the departed and preached to Adam the Good News that he has paid ransom for the sins of Adam and his children by his sacrifice on the cross and they are redeemed. Since the human soul is spiritually responsive and capable of exercising his free will for spiritual functions, Adam offered himself to be redeemed from the domain of Satan and he and his children were restored to Paradise as witnessed by St. Peter (I Pet. 3:18, 19). The marvellous deed of the Divine Saviour who went down to Hades and saw Adam in his place of bondage under Satan, and redeemed him and his descendants from there, is exalted by the human race as the most heroic and unparalleled act in the entire history of the universe and glorified as the most triumphant manifestation of Heavenly love bestowed upon the whole world.

Lord the risen Saviour Said
To Adam in bondage of Hades
Worry no more about your sin
For all that have I paid ransom
The thrashes I took on thy behalf
Were for thy pardon and relief
Forbidden fruit of Eden you ate
Bitter I tasted for its appease
Leaves you got to cover up bare
But me they hung up fully bare
Truly by blood I shed for thee
Annulled Father's wrath on thee

Entry into the Lost Paradise

About this St. Peter says "For Christ died for sins once and for all, a good man on behalf of sinners, in order to lead you to God. He was put to death physically but made alive spiritually and in his spiritual existence, he went and preached to the imprisoned spirits" (I Peter 3:18, 19). "These were the spirits of those who had not obeyed God when He waited patiently during the days when Noah was building his ark. The few people in the ark — eight in all were saved by the water, which was a symbol pointing to Baptism, which now saves you. It is not washing off of bodily dirt, but the promise made to God from a good conscience. It saves you through the resurrection of Jesus Christ" (1st Peter 3:20, 21). Those other people who were not obedient were not saved as Noah and his family. Though God was waiting patiently for them, because of their unbelief (1st Peter 3:19), they were not saved by water but perished in it. But by their death without leaving them to eternal damnation by not getting an opportunity for repentance and deliverance, Christ offered to deliver their souls also by his resurrection as St. Peter writes in his epistle. "It saves you through the resurrection of Jesus Christ, who has gone to Heaven and is at the right side of God, ruling over all angels and Heavenly authorities and powers" (I Peter 3:22) Again see chapter 4:5. "But they will have to give an account of themselves to God who is ready to judge the living and the dead. That is why the Good News was preached also to the dead." Notice how meaningful these verses are as they enlighten how great and sustaining are the love and concern of God regarding the human souls which pass into the Life After Death even though they were disobedient in their life on the earth.

God's Righteousness in Granting an Opportunity to all Mankind as Given to Adam

From the above, it is evident that in the Life After Death, before judgement, to give an opportunity to the departed souls, Christ in the glory of his resurrection, descended into the midst of the departed souls waiting in captivity of Satan in Hades, to preach the Gospel of Salvation and to redeem them to Paradise. Though the earthly life ends with death of the physical body, the human soul continues to live related to God. The wonderful phenomenon is that the free will of man co-exists with the soul even in the Life After Death of the physical body. Therefore with regard to spiritual matters the soul is continuing as thought-luminous in eternity also. This is a state in which the free willed mind can prevail upon the soul to accept or reject the redeeming Gospel of Christ, repent and change the heart or not. In the climax of the transparency of the spiritual world, all the descendants of Adam get the ability and opportunity to review all the acts performed while in the life on earth, whether good or bad, in a well-illuminated self-examination. Since this is a period of Mercy, the like of which was granted to those disobedient people of Noah's time up to the Day of Judgement, the entry of Christ into the Hades is meaningful and becomes causative for the invoking of the grace of redemption from Hades to Paradise. (More details regarding this period of growth and progress in spiritual life, is given later in the discussion of "The Grace of Justification acquired for carrying to the Life After Death" in Chapter 6, pp. 104-06).

The Gospel Granting the Grace of Propitiation of Sins Even After Death

See I Peter 4:5. "But they will have to give account of themselves to God who is ready to judge the living and the dead. That is why the Good News was preached also to the dead." *This is a precious part of the Holy Bible which reveals the heart of Christ.* Foreseeing the possibilities of condemnation of human souls in the Last Judgement due to their evil deeds, it was for giving them the grace of Salvation by his own blood, satisfying God's righteousness in the dictum that "without shedding of blood is no remission of sin" (Heb. 9:22), that Christ went into the Hades to preach the Good News of redemption achieved by the merit of his blood shed in sacrifice on the cross, just as to those living in temporal bodies.

As we see that the departed souls, from Adam up to Christ's death on the cross and His entry into the Hades, who believed in him were saved and redeemed into Paradise, even though their earthly life ended earlier, it behoves that the grant of the grace of remission of sins during the period of Mercy was not denied to them who were in Hades till Christ's entry there. But the Last Judgement is a great decisive event that is going to happen in the future. Then, could anybody expect to find two kinds of justice from the Lord of all righteousness? (1) One justice in the case of Adam and his descendants till Christ's crucifixion and entry into Hades, giving them opportunity in Hades to repent and be saved and (2) A different justice for those who enter eternity after crucifixion refusing them the opportunity in Hades to repent and discarding them to be lost? (See the parable of hiring labourers to the vineyard Mat. 20:1-16. Equal dispensation irrespective of who comes earlier or later). "Don't I have the right to do as I wish with my own money? Or are you jealous because I am generous?" (Mat. 20:15).

Not only among those of whom it was not possible in this world to know about Christ or to believe in him or come into his way of Salvation, but also even among those who are already in the faith, who can claim to have attained the standard of perfection as said by the Lord Jesus Christ? The Lord said: "You must be perfect — just as your father in Heaven is perfect" (Matt 5:48). "But we are all as an unclean thing and all our righteousness are as filthy rags and we all do fade as a leaf; and our iniquities like the wind, have taken us away" (Isaiah 64:6). We get the gift of Salvation only by the grace of God. "For it is by God's grace you have been saved through faith. It is not the result of your own efforts, but God's gift, so that no one can boast about it" (Ephes. 2:8, 9). Therefore Lord Jesus, who has made possible the redemption of all the human beings world over, irrespective of any time, without any discrimination of whether Christians or non Christians, appears to their souls in the Life After Death and grants the gift of Salvation to those who believe in him, and they receive the grace of soul-purification by faith and repentance during the period of Mercy till the Last Judgement. This divine truth is worthy of belief: (Please see more details regarding this in Chapter 6 "Till the Last Judgement Day is the Period of Mercy," p. 106).

The Refuge and Hope in the Life After Death

It is a fact according to the Holy Bible as revealed to us by the Holy Spirit through St. Peter the apostle that, because of the declaration of the Good News of Salvation in Hades many souls believed in Christ and are being saved even now. Jesus Christ, even when he is the omnipresent Son of God, sits at the right hand of God and is offering intercession for us (Rom. 8: 34). Jesus Christ who, showing the blood from the wounds before the Father and pleading for the forgiveness of our sins, is the greatest hope and refuge of mankind, especially in the Life After Death. "And so he is able now and always to save those who come to God through Him because he lives forever to plead with God for them" (Heb 7:25). So, to receive the grace of Salvation one should enter into the fellowship of Holy Spirit and get His guidance. ". . . no man can say Jesus is the Lord but by the Holy Spirit" (I Cor. 12:3).

Non-Christians are also Entitled to Salvation by Faith

There are people who are nominally Christians by being born in a Christian family. There are people who are lucky to have become Christians through the missionary services of the Church. But how many billions of people are there who could not come to this fellowship through any means mentioned above? God who is concerned about and grieved in his divine love for the billions and billions of human souls, who after the earthly life enter eternity from time to time, has expressed his concern in many ways. "There are other sheep which belong to me that are not in this sheep pen. I must bring them too, they will listen to my voice and they will become one flock with one shepherd" (John 10:16). We shall try to understand the great secrets of the redemption that is going on in Hades even now in the light of the love that saves, as expressed in the declaration of Christ cited above. Indeed, the guiding and caring of Christ the Good Shepherd who said "I have the keys of hell and of death" (Rev. 1:18) should be understood more meaningfully with respect to the souls not only in Paradise but also in Hades. This is evidenced from the redemption of souls of the dead from Hades by his entry there as well as the promise to the sinner who repented and acknowledged his faith from the cross. Prophet Isaiah, spiritually visualizing this marvel of God's redemption of souls from Hades, says about it: "I will also give thee for a light to the Gentiles, that thou mayest be my salvation unto the end of the earth" (Isaiah 49:6). Christ is the pre-existent Messiah. (See International Bible Commentary: p. 1052-3). "And he is the propitiation for our sins: and not for our's only but also for the sins of the whole world" (I John 2:2).

Jesus Christ commending the faith of the Roman Centurion who said "Lord I am not worthy that thou shouldst come under my roof; but speak the word only and my servant shall be healed," (Matt. 8:8), marvelled and said: "Verily I say unto you, I have not found so great faith, no, not in Israel." He continued: "That many shall come from east and west and shall sit down with Abraham, Isaac and Jacob in the kingdom of Heaven. But the children of the kingdom shall be cast into outer darkness" (Matt. 8:10-12). Christ has said very clearly: "Not everyone that sayeth unto me, Lord, Lord, shall enter into the kingdom of heaven; but he that doeth the will of My

Father which is in heaven. Many will say to me in that day, Lord, Lord, have we not prophesised in thy name? and in thy name have we cast out devils? and in thy name done many wonderful works? And then will I profess unto them, I never knew you: depart from me, ye that work iniquity" (Matt. 7:21-23). Those who profess as saved and redeemed children, due to their poverty in genuine faith and in excellence of righteous deeds, do not acquire the grace of justification. The allusion here is that the gentiles who assemble from different corners of the earth will get the grace of justification by genuine faith as mentioned above. Humble and contrite hearts will receive the grace of justification by deeds and faith and become worthy of the kingdom of Heaven.

In this connection it is relevant what Christ said to the chief priests and elders of the people who came unto him questioning his authority to teach: "Verily I say unto you that the publicans and the harlots go into the Kingdom of God before you" (Matt. 21:31). Jesus explains why so, as in the next verse. That is: when John the Baptist preached in the way of righteousness they repented and received the grace of justification by faith, but even after seeing it the chief priests and elders of the people have not repented and believed (Matt. 21:32).

Christ the redeemer of the world, who knows that the human soul has got a free willed mind that is able to receive the Good News of Salvation through His sacrifice of propitiation for sins and acquire the grace of Salvation, is conveying the Gospel of redemption to it before the Day of Last Judgement. The divine love and the grant of redeeming grace are deep spiritual secrets; the living Holy Spirit is marvellously working in it. Every soul will pass through either Paradise or Hades, depending on its righteous or unrighteous life on earth, and there Christ will appear to every soul offering the last chance to avail of the redemption through his sacrifice.

Baptism of Salvation from Water and Spirit — Spiritual Re-Birth in Earthly life and Life After Death

What is mentioned in p. 73, under the caption "Entry of Christ into Hades" that the Salvation of Noah and his family from deluge was "a symbol pertaining to Baptism," is more relevant here. As seen in I Peter 3: 20-21, "*Baptism for Salvation is not washing off of bodily dirt, but the promise to God from a good conscience.* It saves you through the resurrection of Jesus Christ." Jesus Christ taught by his own example in undergoing baptism by John the Baptist, that it is required to fulfill all righteousness, both divine and human, and that to be born again it is essential for us to be baptised by water and spirit. *But for those who could not get Baptism like that, in their life in this world, in the Life After Death, having no physical body, they cannot get baptised by water. Baptism with water signifies the invoking of invisible grace through visible means. Marvellous are the ways of God. The symbol pertaining to baptism mentioned above should be understood in its proper sense of application.* See the typological sacramental* interpretation of St. Paul: I Cor. 10:1-2: "*Our ancestors . . . in the cloud and in the sea were baptised as followers of Moses." Cloud and sea are taken together and refer to baptism. Also see how the malefactor, who repented and believed in Jesus Christ as redeemer, was given the promise of being with Christ in Paradise.* See Acts 11: 16-18, *as "What the Lord had said: John baptised with water, but you will be baptised by the Holy Spirit. It is clear that God gave those Gentiles the same gift that he gave us when we believed on the*

---

* The International Bible Commentary, p. 1692.

Lord Jesus Christ; who was I then, to try to stop God!. . . ." "Then God has given to the Gentiles also the opportunity to repent and live!" See Christ's concern for the imprisoned spirits of even those who had not obeyed God when he waited patiently during the days that Noah was building his boat (I Pet. 3:20). Like that it can be assured that those who believe in Christ in the Life After Death also will be worthy of Salvation and will be able to live in Paradise. Even in the case of believers though it was not possible to reach perfection (Matt. 5:48) which the Heavenly Father seeks to find in us, those who have sincerely endeavoured to reach that goal, will receive in the Life After Death the gift of grace to attain Salvation through justification by faith, "And in his name shall the gentiles put their hope" (Matt.12:21) because, "A bruised reed shall he not break and the smoking flax shall he not quench" (Isaiah 42:3 & Matt. 12:20). More details in this connection are given in the discussion under the caption "Justification by Faith is the Hope in the Life After Death" (Chapter 6, pp. 108-10 & Chapter 9, pp. 122-25).

Work of the Holy Spirit that Prevails in the Life After Death

The secrets of the way in which God reveals His love towards human souls are very deep and beyond comprehension. For those who are living in this world and for those who enter the life eternal, the gift of grace would be granted as deserved by each individual. The secrets thereof are beyond the comprehension of human mind. In the Life After Death, the grant of grace of being born again by spiritual Baptism for Salvation of the soul is through the mysterious works of the Holy Spirit's profound saving secrets. For us to get an approximate idea about it, Jesus Christ has said as in a parable: "The wind blows wherever it wishes; you hear the sound it makes, but you do not know where it comes from or where it is going. It is like that with everyone who is born of the Spirit (John 3:8).

Dr. Stanley Johnes who was the permanent speaker for several years at the Maramon convention in Kerala, in one of his sermons said that he cannot imagine a Heaven without Mahatma Gandhi. This statement raised the brow of many people then. But a highly learned theologian and a wholly devoted Christian Dr. Stanley Jhones was expounding there the above-mentioned fact. Even in the Life After Death the influence and intercommunion of the Holy Ghost would be purifying human souls and renovating the spiritual life. The souls of the faithful departed in the Church Expectant waiting in Paradise are also deriving the benefit of this and getting more purified by the true and spiritual worship of God, growing from grace to grace and becoming sanctified and worthy of Heaven.

Souls which do not Get Propitiation of Sins Even in the Life After Death

"If you confess that Jesus is Lord and believe that God raised Him from death, you will be saved. For it is by our faith that we are put right with God; it is by our confession that we are saved" (Rom 10:9-10). The souls in Paradise are the ones which have proved their faith through actual deeds while in their earthly life. Before God, their life was the real worship in spirit and truth.

The confession that "Jesus is the Lord" can come out only from a truly faithful heart. It is not simply vain expression through any utterance by mouth. Also it is not simply any utterance that saves. It should have the strength of a true life of absolute faith in God. Such a faith will have the strength by merit of good deeds of righteousness and love shining out in life. Life on earth has to be an expression of true worship of God in spirit and truth. This life of faith continues as an unending spiritual ecstasy in the Life After Death resulting in the thrilling experience of worshipping God in eternity. Salvation by faith is the substance of evidence in Life After Death. "No one can please God without faith" (Heb. 11:6). "Now faith is the substance of things hoped for, the evidence of things not seen" (Heb. 11:1). The love of God kindles faith in human souls that worship Him, and enlightens them to visualize His Glory. Isaiah had such a vision of the Lord (Isaiah 6: 1-10). Seeing the Lord, Isaiah realized his unworthiness. In adoring God's glory, Isaiah is confronted by His august theophany and becomes conscious of his uncleanliness. That causes repentance and contrition. Then the seraph touches his lips with a burning coal, takes away the iniquity, and sin is purged. Worship of God has such beneficial effect of sanctification of souls to inherit Heaven. If the souls do not carry the habit of worshipping God into the Life After Death, they cannot get remission of sins.

Worldly Life in which Shines the Faith in Action

Let us take an example: In the prayer which our lord taught us, we pray "Give us this day our daily bread." A person who utters this prayer following the praise "Glory be to thee God, my creator," fully believes that God is his creator and that God who is pleased with his sincerity in carrying out his duties, will meet his daily needs and sustain him well. It is evident that his faith in God is quite a living faith and his life is faith-animated throughout. On the contrary, without performing one's duties honestly and sincerely and thinking that he cannot survive unless he indulges in unrighteous ways to enhance his income by adopting any corrupt and foul means, his faith in the God who sustains his life, becomes dead. It is a true fact that, without faith in God, so essential for Salvation, there is no use in mere utterances. It will be pleasing to God only if the faith in God shines out in practical life as a living force of inspiration, pervading through all details of the earthly life. Even in the Life After Death, it would be counted as acquired glory of character of the soul to make it worthy of the grace required for Salvation.

Blasphemy Against the Holy Spirit — If the Conscience is Paralysed by Self-justification and Hardened without Compunction

After leading a reckless life, suppressing the conscience that should be kept uncorrupt and indulging in self-willed life not pleasing to God, nobody needs to think about repenting in the Life After Death and be saved. The one malefactor who was crucified alongside Christ and passed through all the same sufferings, for reason of his conscience had become lifeless and unable to feel any remorse for his evil deeds could not believe in Jesus Christ nor could get the promise of Paradise. He too had the desire to be saved. Still, what did he say from his cross? "If thou be Christ, save thyself and us" (Luk. 23: 39). What filthy words of ridicule! "If thou be Christ" indicates absolutely no faith. For the soul with conscience hardened by the sin of blasphemy and not having any contrition or faith, will not have the preparedness to believe in the Gospel of Salvation or to derive its benefits. From this incident it is clear that a soul, the conscience of which is deadened without any feeling of compunction, will not get the grace to acquire the saving faith or its benefits. That is a state in which the conscience is hardened by self-justification, and sealed against the influence of the Holy Ghost to produce effects of contrition and its benefits. It is about this condition, the Lord Jesus Christ has said: "Wherefore I say unto you all manner of sin and blasphemy shall be forgiven unto men; but blasphemy against the Holy Ghost shall not be forgiven unto men" (Matt. 12:31), (Mark 3:28-29) & (Luk.12:10). This condition of mind in a human soul carries it to the path of Hell as explained in Chapter 11 on Hell, pp. 182-84.

6

Worship and Intercessory Prayer in the Earthly Life and in the Life Thereafter

MAN has in his soul the ability to converse with God at any time and at any place, as the soul is the creation of God. This is the birthright of any human being in the world, irrespective of caste, creed, nationality or language. Let us have a close and deep study about this as it is a glorious characteristic of the soul that goes along with it into the Life After Death.

In the Earthly Life

There are three constituents in the human being — Body, Mind and Spirit (Soul). In these, if the body is a material object, the mind and spirit are invisible forces that abide in the body. But spirit is the life force. The mind, always in co-operation with the spirit acts as a motive force in the different activities of life. The mind and spirit are sharing and co-operating in all activities of human life.

Faith and Theophanic Revelations in Human Mind

The most glorious activity in which a human mind can engage in is the worship of God. In this the body also co-operates to a certain limited extent with the mind and the soul. The love and faith in God enshrined and strengthened in man's heart emboldens him to call upon God, his creator and sustainer, as "My God." By the freedom of love and confidence of faith in God, man's soul began to imbibe and cherish the divinely inspired acquiescence to God's theocratic sovereign laws and divine commands. This holy inspiration of spiritual fellowship with God, who is the supreme spirit, was confidently preserved as a birthright by such of the men who were swayed by the Holy Spirit through the ages. But only a few distinct persons like saints, prophets etc. in the different regions and cultures were favoured with Theophanic revelations.* (*"An unending line of masters of God-realisation, expressing their own subjective experience of the Divinity that is All-pervading, are the various Upaniṣads which form the third book of each Veda"*) (*Hindu religion*) — *These exceptional spiritual luminaries were initiating religious thoughts about divinity and hope of salvation in humans throughout the world in human history through ages, as mentioned in Heb, 1:1: "God who at sundry times and in diverse manners spake in time past unto the fathers by the prophets."*

"Then said I, Lo, I come in the volume of the book it is written of me."(Psal. 40:7). Again see the Epistle to Hebrews 10:7 "Then said I "Lo, I come (in the volume of the book it is written of me) to do thy will O God." Jesus identified himself with the relevant portion from the prophesy of Isaiah Chapter 61 as witnessed in the Gospel of St. Luke 4: 14-21. *The early Judeo Christian scripture "Pentateuch" written by the first prophet Moses begins from about 4000 BC. The Hindu "Vedas" and "Upaniṣads" also originated from about that depth of time. These are the Theophanic revelations of Holy Spirit to prophets, focusing on a universal saviour for the fallen humanity. The Holy Spirit has been influencing human minds through millenniums in "diverse manners" in the different faiths in different regions of the world to the true faith.* This was according to a divine plan to send a

---

* Note: *Kaṭhopaniṣad*, p. 72 (English version by Swamy Chinmayananda).

saviour to redeem the human souls from the curse of sin to the presence of God in a glorious life after their earthly life. From millenniums before the birth of Christ, the enlightened Hindus were hallowing the name of Vedic "Prajāpati" the promised redeemer in their daily worship by reciting "Śrī Viṣṇu Sahasranāmam": Adoration 9, 21 and "Namavali" 69. The devoted and prominent wise men and kings of the orient, guided by the divine light that heralded the birth of Jesus Christ on Christmas night, trekked all the way from the East (India) to Bethlehem to behold and adore him (Matt. 2:1, 9, 10, 11), even though the Jews could not recognize their promised Messiah. After the death of Christ on the cross (wooden sacrificial post as said in *Ṛgveda* X: 90:7), St. Thomas the apostle was sent by the resurrected Christ himself to India to spread the Good News of salvation. Then the Orthodox brāhmaṇas of Kerala, the Namboodiris who were true worshippers of "Prajāpati" had no difficulty to identify Jesus Christ as the promised saviour mentioned as "Prajāpati" in the *Ṛgveda* and *Itharayopaniṣad*. So they believed in him and embraced Christianity and established churches for worship.** (St. Paul states in Rom. 10:9. "If thou shalt confess with thy mouth the Lord Jesus, and shalt believe in thine hearts that God hath raised him from the dead, thou shall be saved." These learned men had no difficulty to identify this with the statement in the *Ṛgveda* X: 90:16 "Those who worship him (Chanting with lip, believing in the heart) get liberation in this world itself and there is no other way besides for salvation." Thus the Holy Spirit of God worked through Theophanic revelations quite harmoniously linking humanity from different regions and in "diverse manners" as mentioned in Heb. 1:1.

** Ref: para 4 & 5, p. 33 of book *Divine Harmony* by Aravindaksha Menon.

The Concept of worship of God and prayer thus established and developed in different parts of the world among people of different religions and cultures have taken diverse forms and yet the consensus was to keep up the spiritual link of man with God for receiving all necessary graces. This common and universal link of different religious philosophies centered on God, is religious harmony in the entire world and really religious people are happy in preserving it. Further, inspired by divine love, just as they were praying for themselves, people, irrespective of any religious denomination, began to pray for others also in intercession, for their bodily as well as spiritual needs. Sitting in one continent and praying in intercession for some beloved one in another continent, we find solace in invoking the Grace of God on our beloved ones. If that is a miraculous act, the ability of the human soul for this purely spiritual exercise in praying for the benefit of others, in earthly life or Life After Death, is undoubtedly a credible fact and a superb experience. If we deny help to a poor man at a time when it is most needed or trouble him in any way, then remember, the cry of his soul will reach God his Creator (Deut. 15:9). If we see a poor man hungry and feed him, we are acting on behalf of God who has to sustain that man's life. God does not appear in material body to do such services. So His divine love prompts human souls for such services.

Thus His will is done through us. That shows the divine connection human souls have got with the Divinity of God and the ability for rendering such common place services of temporal nature. This is all the more true in respect of spiritual services also while human souls co-operate with God's sustaining love for His creation.

Thus intercessory prayers, for the benefit of others in spirit and divine love are supremely pleasing to God as selfless services. To be enlightened on services and duties to be rendered to fellowmen around us, we should be diligent in divine worship, adoration, communion with God, intercessory prayers, and study of the Word of God.

In the Life After Death

When the earthly life ends, the soul and the mind leave the body. The lifeless material body turns mud to earth. The soul with the mind is hidden with Christ in God. In that state of separation from the body, the soul with the mind will be in an inseparably joined state to face the Last Judgement. The sphere of activity and the abilities of the soul will be divinely enlarged and enhanced from the mundane level to the Heavenly heights.

Without the limitations of the temporal body the soul gets more vivid sense of the presence of God. To understand how the soul would be engaged in the Life After Death, we have to ponder upon prayers in four varied aspects.

(A) Divine worship and communion with God by the souls of the faithful departed.

(B) Intercessory prayer by the souls of the faithful departed for the dear ones in militant life in the world.

(C) Intercessory prayers by the faithful in this earthly life for the souls of their departed ones for grant of the grace of forgiveness through justification by faith.

(D) Divine communion with God during the life in this world, continuing as deep-felt experience of devotional ecstasy.

These are explained hereunder:

(A) DIVINE WORSHIP AND COMMUNION WITH GOD BY THE SOULS OF THE FAITHFUL DEPARTED

Endless worship of God in Paradise

It is stated earlier that until the great day of resurrection of the dead, the souls of the faithful are hidden with Christ in God (Col. 3:3). They, having been in quite lively individuality, are always worshiping and glorifying God. *For them, there is no limitation of the physical shackles of pain, anxiety and worry. Worship and adoration are their all-time pleasure. The souls which live in Christ who is the source of life, cannot but be worshipping and adoring their creator and redeemer, because of the great love and ardency of faith in him.* For that reason it is impossible for them to be in silence or slumber. The habit of worship that was established in the earthly life is continued unceasingly into the life in Paradise also. Visualising this in spiritual perception, the royal prophet David exalts in his Psalms: "But we will bless the Lord from this time forth and for ever more. Praise the Lord" (Psal. 115:18). "For ever" means in eternity too. The human souls which love God whole- heartedly will be deeply concerned to worship God even in their Life After Death. As the Lord has stated "I am the vine and you are the branches" (John 15:5), only those souls which abide in him and getting spiritual nourishment from him, can have the Heavenly inspiration for that.

There is no Worship of God in the Silent World of the Spiritually Dead. But the Spiritually Alive Worship Him for Ever

Those who are subjugated by sin, who deadened their conscience without any self-examination or repentance, and who have entered Hades without any faith in Christ the Saviour, would be in eternal silence, because they are spiritually dead. "The dead praise not the Lord, neither any that go down into silence."(Psalm. 115:17). In the spiritually dead world of Satan, there is no faith and love and therefore no worship of God. Even while in their life in this world those who have become the servants of Satan, obey him in carrying out his orders to be evil and so would not have the habit of worshipping God. Therefore in the Life After Death also they would not worship God. As a result, there is no spiritual growth. It would be possible only to go on sinking into morbidity of the soul, with the experience of death forced upon them by Satan as the wages due for sins committed while in the physical life. What is stated in Psalms 115:17 quoted above is about the human soul which was in silence without worshipping God even while living in this world. Quoting this verse some people falsely interpret that all who die are silent and are not worshipping God. This is an absurd interpretation of the Holy Word, as it can be clearly seen from what is stated quite unequivocally in the immediately continuing verse as: "But we will bless the Lord from this time forth and for ever more. Praise the Lord" (Psal. 115:18) (Also please see Rev. 7:15). "Therefore are they before the throne of God and serve him day and night in his temple and he that sitteth on the throne shall dwell among them."

Worship in Spirit and Truth in the Life on Earth and the Life After Death

"God is a spirit: and they that worship him must worship him in spirit and truth" (John 4:24). *Those who live in this physical world should primarily attune themselves spiritually to be in harmony with the spirit of God to acquire the ability to receive him and derive the divine happiness of communion with Him. "Abide in Me, and I in you"* (John 15:4). *"Those who worship Me with devotion, they are in Me and I also am in them"* (*Bhagavad Gītā*: Ch. IX, Verse 29).

This act is not bound by time or space and the solace knows no bounds in spiritual transcendence.* "As God is, so is his worshipper." This exalted experience is defined in the Hindu philosophy as "*Tat Tvam Asi*" meaning "You and I are one."**

At this stage, the worshipper realises the truth, i.e. God alone can give the spirit of oneness with him. He alone has the spirit to give to the worshipper, harmony to promote spiritual worship. For that the resurrected Christ ascended to Heaven, with human souls redeemed from the curse of sin. When Christ resurrected and entered the glorious presence of God the Father in Heaven with the sacrificial blood in the wounds of crucifixion atoning for the sins of the whole world, he carried the redeemed mankind in Sonship with him. It was the manifestation of what He said: "I am the Way, the Truth and the Life" (John 14:6). It was this fact that he revealed to the Samaritan woman "Believe me. The hour cometh, when you shall neither in this mountain nor yet at Jerusalem, worship the Father" (John 4:21). "But the hour cometh, and now is, when the true worshippers shall worship the Father in spirit and truth: For the Father seeketh such to worship Him" (John 4:23). The Holy Spirit is the spirit of truth. Through him the grace of Jesus Christ is ours and therefore, the worship in spirit is worship in truth. This is beyond time and space and therefore is true in the Life After Death also as in the earthly life.

---

* "With Christ in the School of prayer" — by Andrew Murray, p. 11, Nisbet & Co. Ltd., 22 Berners Street, London W. 1, 1885.

** ("That thou art" — In prose order it is "Thou art That." The purport of this sublime sentence is that you are not alien to God. In some form or other this idea is contained in all scriptures. The *Bhagavad Gītā* is from beginning to end a grand commentary on this sublime statement — Thou art That). Ref: "Introduction to *Bhagavad Gītā*" by Swami Chidbhavananda, p. 40, Thapovan Publishing House, Tirupparāitturai, P.O., Tiruchirappalli Dist. Tamil Nadu, 1967.

In the Life After Death, without the confines of the earthly body, it is possible for human souls to realize these facts very clearly in the high transparency of the spiritual world. Then, those who had a life of faith in this world, in which the real truth was shining out from the core of their hearts in genuine love towards God, will continue in the worship of God in spirit and truth in eternity also.

Worship of God is Grace-Responsive

While enjoying the good gifts God has provided for our necessities of life and happiness, how many of us realise the divine love that has made available those things? Getting immersed in vain pleasures, filling the heart with the gifts rather than the giver, forgetting God or living without much concern about God, is what happens even among many so-called believers. But beyond the worldly vanities, in the Paradise of solace, where it is possible to realise more about God and the glorious things God's love has provided for human souls, there would be an ardent desire from within to offer praise and adoration over and over again before God. David, foreseeing the paradisal life where love and faith in God abound, exalts in his Psalms "One thing have I desired of the Lord, that will I seek after; that I may dwell in the house of the Lord all the days of my life, to behold the beauty of the Lord, and to enquire in his temple" (Psalms 27:4). "When thou saidst, "Seek ye my face; my heart said unto thee, Thy face, Lord, will I seek" (Psal. 27:8). See how David responds:

Therefore, to be worthy of the grant of grace by worship of God in the Life After Death, it is very necessary to acquire the habit of worshipping God even while in this life itself, as observed by David. The habit is continued by the soul in the Life After Death as explained above.

Universality of Worship is Better Understood in the Life After Death

The human soul comes to realize many spiritual truths only when it gets free from the vain shackles of this world. One such spiritual truth is the universality of the worship of God. That is, the worship of the human beings in this world, worship of the faithful departed souls and worship of the Heavenly hosts of angels in the world beyond, are all equally acceptable before God. The faithful departed, having the habit of worshipping the true God in what-ever form, as they are in spiritual body while in eternity, cannot but be eye-witnesses and partakers in the spiritual and true worship going on there. In the vision Isaiah had in the spiritual ecstasy (Isaiah 6:1-8) saw God sitting on the Heavenly throne and the hosts of angels worshipping him. Then Isaiah who gets immersed in that spiritual experience gets a change of heart and remission of sins. Along with that, he gets a mandate from God coupled with spiritual strength to carry it out. We see Isaiah coming out with renewed strength to his life of service as prophet of the Lord. This is an example of how a person in the habit of worshipping God even while in the earthly life, gets spiritual abilities equivalent to spiritual beings. Experience of the spirits of the faithful who enter the Life After Death is also the same. Therefore the fact that the worship and adoration of God by the spirits of the departed will be acceptable before God along with that of the holy angels, would be realised by the souls in the Life After Death.

Development of Spiritual Life Experienced in the Spiritual Worship of Paradise

The spirits of the faithful who are in Christ are growing ever more in the luxuriant life in Paradise. Where there is life there is growth also. Spirits of the faithful are called from the Church

Militant where they are engaged in a relentless fight against the world, flesh (human bodily nature) and Satan, to eternity to await the Last Judgement. ". . . . We are not of them who draw back unto perdition; but of them that believe to the saving of the soul" (Heb 10:39). "I am the vine, ye are the branches; He that abideth in me, and I in him, the same bringeth forth much fruit: for without me, ye can do nothing" (John 15:5). The above word of Christ is proof that the spirits of the departed who are hidden with Christ in God, are to receive life in plenty from Christ the real vine to bear much spiritual fruit. Bearing fruit is clear evidence of growth. The grace necessary for such spiritual growth is granted because of worshipping and adoring God always. Therefore in the Life After Death, the prime activity of the soul is worship of God resulting in spiritual growth.

Prayer Enjoined with Worship in the Life After Death

Along with the worship of human souls in the earthly life, there would be prayer for matters concerned with the needs for their living. That prayer would be according to the will of God. See how the beloved Lord, in the prayer he taught us, has added the request for our daily bread for the bodily need, and protection from temptation for the spiritual safety! The souls, in the Life After Death, not having material body, would not have any bodily needs. Therefore there is no necessity for them to pray for such necessities of earthly life. But it is necessary and appropriate to pray earnestly along with worship for the necessary grace to grow to perfection. "Be ye therefore perfect, even as your Father in Heaven is perfect." (Matt. 5:48) "For God so loved the world that he gave his only begotten son, that whosoever believeth in him should not perish, but have everlasting life" (John 3:16). ". . . It is Christ that died, yea, rather, that is risen again, who is even at the right hand of God, who also maketh intercession for us" (Rom 8:34).

"Wherefore he is able also to save them to the uttermost that come unto God by him, seeing he ever liveth to make intercession for them" (Heb 7:25). In such an assured faith it is quite appropriate and graceful that the departed souls in their worship of God pray for their spiritual life and growth towards perfection which our father in Heaven wants to find in us.

(B) INTERCESSION BY THE FAITHFUL DEPARTED FOR THE BELOVED IN THE WORLD

Most Exalted Prayer of Intercession Even in the Life After Death

One need not have any doubt about the efficacy of intercession, the most exalted prayer in the Life After Death. The prompting spirit in this is the living Holy Spirit of God abiding in the faithful. When he was laid on the cross and his palms were nailed to the cross, when the holy blood sprang out from the wounds began the intercession of "the mediator of the new covenant and to the blood of sprinkling, that speaketh better things than that of Abel" (Heb. 12:24). In the souls of the faithful, who in the Holy Communion* partake Holy Blood and Body, His spirit manifests. Therefore the souls of the faithful who had this characteristic quality of offering intercessory prayers for others in their earthly life, would be offering such prayers in their Life After Death also. Their intercessory prayers also reach before the Father's throne through the mediation of Lord Jesus Christ, the sole mediator for mankind. About offering prayer for physical and spiritual needs before God, along with worship is already explained in the previous paragraph.

---

* A clarification on the great sacramental secret in the believers' partaking Holy Body and Blood of Jesus Christ, is provided later in this chapter).

Even in Life After Death there is Concern About those in the Physical Life

From the parable of Rich man and Lazarus told by the Lord (Luk. 16:27-28) it can be seen that the life problems of the beloved in earthly life are in the attention of the departed souls and they are concerned about it. It is seen that the rich man is requesting father Abraham to send Lazarus to give necessary advice to his five brothers in the earthly life so that they may not come to that place of torment. If a Hell-deserving soul had so much concern about other souls, how much more concerned would be the souls of the faithful departed about the good of their beloved living in this world and be praying in intercession for them.

The Heavenly Vision which Emboldened St. Stephen

Chapter 7 in the book of Acts of the Apostles gives a description of the scene of Jews stoning Stephen to death. Especially verses 55 and 56 are noteworthy. Amidst stones raining on him, "He being full of the Holy Ghost, looked up steadfastly into Heaven, and saw the glory of God, and Jesus standing on the right hand of God. And said, Behold, I see the Heavens opened, and the Son of Man standing on the right hand of God" (Acts 7:55-56).

About what is seen in the vision of Heaven St. Paul hints in his epistle to Hebrews: ". . . we have this large crowd of witnesses around us" (Heb 12:1) and continues on in the words of Moses "The sight was so terrifying — I am trembling and afraid" (Heb 12:21). ". . . . you have come to the Mount of Zion and the city of the Living God, Heavenly Jerusalem, with its thousands of angels. You have come to the joyful gathering of God's first-born sons, whose names are written in Heaven. You have come to God, who is the judge of all mankind and to the spirits of good people made perfect. You have come to

Jesus, who arranged the new covenant and to the sprinkled blood that promises much better things than does the blood of Abel" (Heb. 12:22-24).

"And all that sat in the council, (to condemn Stephen) looking steadfastly on him, saw his face as it had been that of an angel." (Acts 6:15). The Heavenly vision cast such a glorious reflection in his mind. There is such a host of departed souls around us, the faithful, as witnesses of Heavenly fellowship in the spiritual realm, though invisible to us but surely encouraging and emboldening us in our fight against Satan and his hosts. The above-mentioned incident is a proof to show how the souls of our departed ones are lively and always vigilant in a Heavenly mode of existence to help us to victoriously fight against sins and temptations. But this spiritual vision can be seen only with spiritual eyes as those of Stephen.

In the Life After Death the Relationship with the Beloved in the Earthly Life is Continuing without Break in the Oneness with Christ

As seen from the previous paragraphs, because the souls of the departed are concerned about their beloved in the earthly life, the living and the departed are spiritually united in the intercession sharing the expression of love, faith and hope in Christ. "I in them, thou in me, that they may be made perfect in one; and that the world may know that thou hast sent me and hast loved them as thou hast loved me" (John 17:23). As stated above, it is the perfection of the spiritual union that makes the mutual intercession blessed and meaningful. This prayer was not only for the eleven disciples who were gathered there. "Neither pray I for these alone, but for them also which shall believe on me through their word" (John 17:20). In the garden of Gethsemane Jesus Christ prayed for those who are yet to believe in the Gospel, and for the perfect spiritual union, between the faithful and God, without any limitation of place or time. This is the revelation of the assurance and covenant of true love that outlives death and manifests in intercessory prayer in accordance with the Will of God. All intercessory prayers are through the sole mediator Jesus Christ, reaching before God's Throne by the merit of the redemption to Sonship Christ has earned for mankind.

Intercession by the Saints

". . . The effectual fervent prayer of a righteous man availeth much" (James: 5: 16). St. James says this in an exhortation about love-prompted deed of intercession for the good of others. Deeds of love have graceful effect in the spiritual realm even in the life after death. We have ever so many saints declared and undeclared, who lived in this world saintly lives according to the Will of God and entered the life in Paradise from time to time. They are very much involved in communion with God in their Life After Death. "Therefore they are before the throne of God and serve him day and night in his temple; and he that sitteth on the Throne shall dwell among them" (Rev. 7:15). The faithful who are in the militant church in this world, when they are spiritually communing with God in secret prayer, are in fellowship with the spirits of such saintly people who are also in communion with God the father of all. There is no difference of place or time as the spiritual realm is beyond all that. The faithful departed having partaken of the Holy Blood and Body of Christ, and now in the spiritual state, would naturally identify themselves with the vicarious intercession of the Lord Jesus Christ. There are very many sanctifying graceful benefits of this. The beneficiaries of the most glorious graces may not usually speak out on these, as they revere the immaculate ecstasy of the very secrets of the after-death spiritual exercises of the venerable departed parents whose memories are regarded with high esteem. Though these saintly persons pray in intercession to Christ for us and with us, they are not to be identified as mediators for us. Each one of us should cherish an utmost intimate personal relationship with Christ as He is the sole mediator who bequeathed to us the grace of Sonship of God through his sacrifice for us. Intercessory prayer is the spiritually vibrant expression of mutual love among the children of God in the great family of the Heavenly Father, but it is only subservient to Christ's mediation that continues in Heaven for the quick and the departed. Saints are humans just like us who join us in spiritual worship of God and pray for us in intercession through Jesus Christ.

Efficacy of the intercession of St. Mary and other declared saints and even our parents and beloved faithful ones, so much exalted by the Orthodox and Catholic Churches throughout the world, has to be understood in the light of the explanation given above. The loving and helping nature of St. Mary as revealed in a very specific incident in the earthly life of our Lord Jesus Christ, narrated in the Gospel of St. John in Ch. 2: 1-11, casts divine light on this point. Mary, mother of Jesus, while attending a wedding feast of a family at Cana in Galilee, noticed that "they have no wine left" (John 2:3). To run out of wine at a Jewish wedding feast is a very serious matter of shame to the hosting family. Mary, mother of Jesus, seized of the gravity of the situation, brought it to the notice of Jesus, who she thought, would save the situation. That was perhaps the first-ever intercession of the mother to her son on behalf of a family in trouble, evidently to help them.

Note what Jesus says: "My time is not yet come" (John 2:4). What does it mean? It requires an approval. He has to wait for the accord of the Father's Will. Matters moved fast as evidenced by the actions that followed. The Heavenly Father was pleased at the performance of the first miracle to reveal Christ's glory (John 2:11). The servants filled six stone water-jars at the bidding of the mother. Meanwhile Jesus knew of the approval of the Heavenly Father as the time has come. The water filled in the jars was turned into wine by Jesus.

The mother, even now, is in the same helping spirit towards needy people, pleading with her son for helping them, whether they approach her or not. In this case, no request from the family seems to have been made to the mother. It was the mother who observed the awkward situation in which the family was involved and pleaded with Jesus. It is recorded that the man in charge of the feast did not know where this wine came from (John 2:9). So, it is very encouraging for the needy that approach the mother in the hope of pleading with her son, as they also pray to Jesus Christ for grace to get over any difficulty or relief from any suffering. In the same manner those who are in need, will be greatly benefited by their faith by joining in intercessory prayer in spiritual fellowship with the many beloved faithful in this earthly life as well as in the life after life. Prayer being a spiritual exercise, reaches out into the spiritual world too. "The Lord heareth the prayers of the righteous (Prov. 15: 29).

In the Spirit of Adoption of Humanity to Sonship

However, the teaching of the Churches regarding the intercessory prayers of St. Mary and other saintly spirits should not be misconceived as a subway to God besides Jesus Christ who is the only mediator between man and God. The Holy Spirit of God, who guides us in all truth and righteousness, is in unison with God the Father and the Son in the most glorious spiritual exercise of intercession also.

Though the word Trinity is not mentioned anywhere in the Bible, the divine love and concern of these supreme personalities can be seen most harmoniously expressed in dealing with the spirit of man. Especially in the intercessory prayer, the Holy Spirit perfectly links the humanity to God the Father through Jesus Christ the Son, in the spirit of adoption. Let us adore the Holy Trinity.

"For ye have not received the spirit of bondage again to fear; but ye have received the Spirit of Adoption whereby we cry Abba, Father" (Rom 8:15). "Likewise the Spirit also helpeth our infirmities: for we knoweth not what we should pray for as we ought: But the Spirit itself maketh intercession for us with groanings which cannot be uttered" (Rom: 8:26). "And he that searcheth the hearts knoweth what is the mind of the spirit, because he maketh intercession for the saints according to the will of God" (Rom. 8:27). "And we know that all things work together for good to them that love God, to them who are the called according to His purpose" (Rom 8:28). So the intercessory prayers of the holy departed for their beloved in the earthly life are in harmony with the Will of God as in His purpose for their Salvation.

The Divine Love Bonds of the Members of the Great Family of which God is the Father

While the truly faithful pray in the very holy moments of their communion with God in secret prayer rooms of their homes, their supplications reach before the Throne of God in Heaven. The spirits of the saints, which can understand in spirit, will join with abounding love and pray in intercession to Christ the sole mediator manifesting the Heavenly love in the great family of God the Father. Holy Qurbana is the most glorious sacrament of redeeming sacrifice, adoration and worship, invoking the grace of peace with God by intercession of Christ.

Further, the daily family worship in homes, individual secret devotional prayers etc. are means of conveying divine graces by spiritual communion, to both the quick and the departed alike. *Intercession is the supreme act of Love.*

The Expectant Souls in Paradise Grow to Perfection by Receiving the Grace of Justification by Faith Through Self-examination, Repentance and Worship of God

It is already stated earlier that those who have lived in this world and continue in the Life After Death in Paradise, are always adoring and worshipping God. Those who believe in the death of Jesus Christ on the Calvary cross for the remission of our sins and his glorious resurrection on the third day, get absolved of their sins by self-examination, repentance and confession, and become worthy of the grace of redemption as they have partaken of* His Holy Body and Blood. They, who thus identify themselves with the redeemer, in their Life After Death, enter the solace of Paradise. Therefore, in harmony with the spirit of Christ they offer intercessory prayers for redemption of their beloved struggling against sin and temptation in the earthly life. However, to live with the Father in Heaven, they have to attain the perfection as said by Jesus Christ (Please see Matt. 5:48).

(C) THE GRACE OF JUSTIFICATION ACQUIRED BY DEEDS CARRIED TO THE LIFE AFTER DEATH AND GRACE OF JUSTIFICATION BY FAITH ACQUIRED THROUGH INTERCESSORY PRAYERS OF THE BELOVED IN THE WORLD

Justification by Deeds Acquired in the Earthly Life

On careful scrutiny of the physical life of people as hinted in the previous para, it is not possible to find in anyone the

* Please see explanation in the paragraphs to follow.

perfection as desired by God. Even if one had the good fortune for self-examination in all details of life until the close of one's life and confess and discard every sin that could be recollected up to the end of life, it is not possible to reach anywhere near the Heavenly perfection which Jesus Christ spoke about as a target which we should aim at. That perfection of the Heavenly father (Mat 5:48) is superb that it is unattainable by any man. How many sinful acts we might have done thinking in a careless attitude that they are alright and derived self-satisfaction in our own righteousness? How many duties and services that should have been rendered might have been carelessly overlooked or inadvertently neglected and left to oblivion, yet remaining in self-satisfaction? In the divine transparency of the spiritual realm, such commissions and omissions over which we have remained complacent, will be revealed as sinful patches on our image of perfection. Of course, as said by Isaiah the prophet: "But we are all as an unclean thing, all our righteousness is as filthy rags" (Isaiah 64:6). Before such revelations, think where our perfection stands. Further, in the divine transparency of the spiritual realm many sins and evasions of responsibilities not seriously considered in the common standard of worldly life will be vividly seen as imperfection of the soul. Therefore it can be understood how imperfect is the merit of our righteousness or sanctified life in making our souls worthy of Heaven. The soul should appear before God not only absolved of all sins but sanctified in absolute perfection of character. It is impossible for any soul to be absolved of sins and be justified by its own action. Similarly, "You see, then, that it is by his actions that a person is put right with God and not by faith alone" (James 2:24). (Here the example of Abraham is quoted. It was through his actions when he offered his son Isaac as sacrifice on the altar, his faith and action worked together; his faith was made perfect through his action). See James 2:21-23. Faith and practice should match.

Till the Final Judgement Day is the Period of Mercy

Some people quote a portion of a verse from the Holy Word (II Cor 5:10) ". . . that every one may receive the things done in his body, according to that he hath done, whether it be good or bad." They argue that Salvation will strictly be according to the merit of one's deed, good or evil, done till physical death, as the period of mercy ends with death. This is quite a wrong conclusion. They do not visualise the graceful period of mercy provided by the merciful Lord in his plan for Salvation of human souls in their Life After Death till the day of Last Judgement. If there is no such provision, who can possibly be saved? Who has got the worthiness to claim the Sonship of God by the merit of his leading a life so pure and perfect as the Holy Father in Heaven as prescribed by Christ (Matt. 5: 48) and to enter that glory through death? It is not possible even for the exponents of this theory. The Holy Word says: "There is no one who is righteous . . . not even one" (Rom.3: 10-12). "For all have sinned and come short of the glory of God" (Rom.3: 23). What is stated on pages 73-77 in Chapter 5 is pertinent here also in point of fact that the period of mercy is provided by the Merciful Lord even after death till the Day of Judgement. The Glory of God unattainable by any utmost righteous life in the physical world has to be invoked by the grace of justification by an intense life of faith in this period of mercy while the soul is in the Church Expectant. It may be in the Hades with its torments inducing self-examination and contrition or in Paradise with its splendour of spiritual worship and sharing the abundant life of Christ (for more details please see pp. 119-24).

Offering atoning means, the merciful God has ordered and established a stay for human souls in Hades or Paradise, to attain the grace of justification by faith. Therefore the souls get an opportunity in the torments of Hades or in the spiritual solace of Paradise, by Christophanic revelations (Para 16 of Ch. 9) that invoke the grace of justification by faith. There the souls get spiritual enlightenment without any limitations of the temporal body, leading to minute and thorough self-examination and repentance to receive justification by faith. It is utter foolishness and a great evil to discard this great opportunity granted by the merciful Lord for providing a period of expectation for invoking the grace of spiritual refinement for redemption of human souls before the Day of Final Judgement. But this does not mean that the life on the earth can be led carelessly to be mended after death. Be warned by what is stated on page 179.

Deliverance from the Deadly Bite of Fiery Serpents.
Foreshadow of Justification by Faith.

The Israelites while traversing the wilderness, spoke against God and Moses and the Lord sent fiery serpents among the people. They bit the people and many people of Israel died (Numbers 21:5-6). They repented and Moses prayed for them. Then Lord told Moses to make a metal serpent and to hang it on a pole so that any one who was bitten by serpents could look at it and be healed. So Moses made a brazen snake and hung it on a pole. Any one who was bitten would look at the brazen serpent and be healed (Numbers 21:9). This incident was the foreshadow of the cross on which Christ was hung for the universal redemption of human race that became liable for spiritual death by sin.

"Christ himself carried our sins in his body to the cross, so that we might die to sin and live for righteousness"

(I Pet. 2:24). He died on the cross, and was buried; resurrected on the third day, ascended unto Heaven, and is now interceding before God the Father showing His Holy Wounds from which shed the Holy Blood for propitiation of the sins of all humanity. Since the absolution for sin is a spiritual grace, it is effective for the spirits of the quick and the dead alike till the Day of the Last Judgement. After the Last Judgement no mediation is open because on that day the fate of the redeemed and the condemned would be decided once for all. Till then is the period of mercy for any one who believes in the redeeming grace of Christ's sacrifice on the cross and acquires the grace of justification by faith for redemption. "Whoever believes on him will not be disappointed" (Rom 10:11). God's message of faith which the apostles preached is: "If you confess that Jesus is Lord and believe that God raised him from death, you will be saved" (Rom 10:9). However, some people misinterpret this promise of Salvation taking it as a blanket provision for automatic remission of all sins of the past, present and future to get Salvation without any repentance or confession of sins and perfect righteousness in life. Not faith alone, deeds are also required for salvation (See para 24 of Ch. 9). To all human souls who are true believers and repentant, He grants the grace for remission of sins and makes them worthy of living with Him in Heaven. It is this Will of God that is fulfilled in the incarnation of the Son of Man and redemption by his death on the cross, as promised to our ancestors (see Luk. 1:54, 69, 70). However, to derive the benefit of the free gift of Salvation one should have true repentance and faith in the redeemer who was crucified for us.

Justification by Faith is the Hope in the Life After Death

By death, the period of one's deed comes to an end. The law is to discipline the life in this world. What St. Paul says is:

"But by means of that commandment sin found its chance to stir up all kinds of selfish desires in me. Apart from law, sin is a dead thing" (Rom 7:8). "When the commandment came, sin sprang to life and I died" (Rom 7:9). He continues: "And the commandment which was meant to bring life in my case brought death" (Rom 7:10). "I don't do the good I want to do, instead I do the evil that I do not want to do. If I do what I don't want to do, this means I am no longer the one who does it; instead it is the sin that lives in me. So, I find this law is at work; when I want to do what is good, what is evil is the only choice I have" (Rom 7: 19-21). However good the people might be, it is impossible to lead a sinless life in this world. At the end of a tumultuous life in this world, while facing death with a conscience in which shines the balance sheet of a sense of guilt as a result of self-examination, one is prone to ask:

Transient world thou why,
Enticed me so much?
Sea of sins, why did thou
Dip me deep so much?

Then how can the human soul get the worthiness to live in Heaven? The way for Salvation in the glorious Life After Death is only one: "Being justified freely by his grace through the redemption that is in Christ Jesus" (Rom 3:24). This grace of redemption is acquired by the human soul in the Life After Death during the period of mercy till the day of Last Judgement. There is no deed for justification in the Life After Death. Therefore the law does not come there in effect as in the physical life on the earth in which the deeds should be strictly guided by the law. "Where is boasting then?" it is excluded. By what law? Of works? Nay: but by the law of faith. Therefore we conclude That a man is justified by faith without deeds of law" (Rom. 3: 27, 28). After a life observing the law of deeds in this world, any man gets the worthiness for life in heaven only with the grace of justification by faith which is the glorious hope in the Life After Death. That is the justifying grace of the redeeming blood of Jesus Christ shed on the Calvary Cross. However, to acquire that, there should be a faithful and deep-felt repentance, spiritual preparedness and prayer on the part of every human being in Paradise or Hades, during the period of mercy.

The Grace of Justification Received by Believers in the Divine Sacrifice that Grants Remission of Sins and Spiritual Life

From Adam up to the death of Christ on the cross, all the human souls who entered the Life After Death, as sinners were caught in the captivity of Satan. Though it was impossible to bridge the great gap between the holiness of God and sin-defiled state of man by means of any propitiating act, for justification by deeds, commandments and law were given to man as disciplinary norms for life. Further, in case of any transgression of the law, in accordance with God's righteousness that "without shedding of blood is no remission" (Heb 9:22), there were various sacrifices and purification ceremonies prescribed in the law given through Moses. "They were symbols which point to the present time. It means that the offerings and animal sacrifices offered to God cannot make the worshippers' heart perfectly sanctified since they have to do only with food, drink and various purification ceremonies.These were all outward ceremonious rules, which apply only until the time when God will establish the new order" (Heb. 9: 9-10). "But now once in the end of the world hath he appeared to put away sin by the sacrifice of himself" (Heb. 9: 26). That is the most perfect sacrifice in which Jesus Christ the God-incarnated Son of Man offered his holy blood on the cross in propitiation of the sins of the whole world.

More details of these covenants of the Holy Eucharist are explained later in this book.

The Holy Qurbana — Sacrificial Worship of the New Testament

On the night previous to Christ's crucifixion, He established the sacrament of the Holy Qurbana in co-ordination with the Jewish festival of Passover. According to the Old Testament, before liberation of Israelites from the slavery of Pharaoh, they were told by the Lord through Moses that they have to kill a lamb and strike its blood on the two side posts and upper door post of their houses and eat the flesh roasted by fire. This was a token observation to ensure the redemption of their first born males from death when the Lord passed that night through Egypt and smote all the first-born of man and beasts to execute judgement. Therefore the Passover was symbolically observed by the Jews through generations commemorating their liberation and redemption from slavery in Egypt. *In the New Testament, Jesus Christ came as the Lamb of God that bore the sins of the whole world offering himself as a propitiating sacrifice on the cross to redeem the whole world.* Therefore, He being the Lamb of God for sacrifice, the old custom of killing a lamb was replaced. Instead He took bread in his hands, blessed it, broke it and gave to his disciples. "Take and eat it." He said: "This is my body." Then He took a cup, gave thanks to God and gave it to them. "Drink it all of you." He said: "This is my blood poured out for many for the forgiveness of sins" (Matt. 26: 26-27), (Mark 14: 22-24), (Luk. 22:19-20). He added: ". . . this do in remembrance of me."(Luk. 22:19). So it is a perpectual memorial. *"Thus when the Church commemorates the Last Supper it is not a mere human effort to recall the past. By obeying the Lord's command to remember, the*

Church participates in the eschatological salvation that the supper and the cross together have brought out" (International Bible Commentary, p. 251). *The application here is that the establishment of the Sacrament of Holy Qurbana by Christ is also for remembrance of him through his sacrifice on the cross as a covenant by which human souls will be remembered in his Kingdom for salvation. The prayer of the repented malefactor crucified with Christ: "Lord, remember me when thou comest into thy Kingdom."* (Luk. 23:42) *was the first Eucharistic prayer that was immediately favoured with a graceful answer: "Today shalt thou be with me in Paradise."* (Luk. 23:43).

Foreshadowing this is the covenant of deliverance from destruction by deluge, visualised in God's love which established the appearance of a rainbow in the clouds by which God would remember the everlasting covenant between Him and all living beings on earth that a flood will never again destroy all living beings (Gen 9: 8-17).

The Bread and Wine Offered in Holy Qurbana the Spiritual Sacrifice

In the Jewish sacrifices according to their law were blood offerings. In the New Testament in the propitiating sacrifice, the sacrificial mass offered is bread and wine, symbolical of Christ's own Body and Blood. It is believed as such because Christ himself said it when he established the sacrament of Holy Qurbana. God who created all by his word, said "This is my body and this is my blood." And so it is. Though there is no visible change in the substance of the mass offered in the sacrifice, as pronounced by the Lord while establishing the Holy Qurbana, by the power of the same Word, the bread and wine are realised by the faithful truly as the holy Body and Blood of Christ. But for those who do not believe in his words that would be only bread and wine. In living reality of this symbol, God incarnate as a perfect man, that is, the Word which became flesh in the virgin was perfectly human. In that condition, for his sustenance in the infantile limitations to which he has condescended, He was fully dependent on his mother, though at the same time He was perfectly God, the creator and sustainer of the entire universe. "For in him dwelleth all the fullness of Godhead bodily."(Col. 2:9). To believe that, it is possible only for those who have the eye of faith. The application of the symbolism here to be understood is that the bread and wine ordained by the Lord as sacrificial mass in the sacrament of the Holy Qurbana, though not visibly showing in its substance any change in colour, taste etc. are realised as the Holy Body and Blood of the Son of Man. Christ's disciples believed so, and so also all the true believers after them, through the ages in the life of the church.

Holy Qurbana the Bread of Life

The concept of offering sacrifices to please God for getting blessings and remission of sins is enshrined in the Old Testament commands and norms prescribed for observations in animal sacrifice. Blood is life which belongs to God. Blood offering in sacrifices was a widespread phenomenon in all religions as of Israel who observed it with divine command. According to the Old Testament there were divine instructions on the form for offering sacrifices. They were a "Meat Offering" (Lev 2:1), a "Sin Offering" (Lev 4:25), a "Trespass Offering" (Lev 5:6), a "Peace Offering" (Lev 7:15) or a "Wave Offering" (Lev 7:30). It was also enjoined that any one on whose behalf the offering is made, should eat a portion of the mass offered. By that only the offering becomes complete and he becomes identified with it. (Lev 2:10, 5:13, 6:16, 20 & 8:31). Since the sacrificial mass offered in the propitiating sacrifice of the New Testament is the holy Body and Blood of the saviour, the faithful for whom it is offered by taking a portion of it becomes identified with the Holy Body and Blood, and invokes the worthiness for receiving the grace of justification by faith. Christ, who prepared the way for redemption to life from death of the soul due to sin, said: "I am the bread of life" (John 6:48). "I am the living bread which came down from Heaven: if any man eat of this bread, he shall live for ever and the bread that I will give is my flesh, which I will give for the life of the world" (John 6:51). He continues: "Verily verily I say unto you, except ye eat the flesh of the Son of Man, and drink his blood, ye have no life in you. Whosoever eateth my flesh and drinketh my blood, hath eternal life; and I will raise him up at that day" (John 6:53, 54). "He that eateth my flesh and drinketh my blood, dwelleth in me and I in him" (John 6:56). "As the living Father hath sent me and I live by the Father; so he that eateth me, even he shall live by me. This is the bread which came down from Heaven; not as your fathers did eat manna and are dead; he that eateth of this bread shall live for ever" (John 6:57, 58). There should be spiritual hunger to take this Bread of Life regularly to keep up the life of our soul strong and healthy to fight against sin and temptation of evil.

Christ's Sacrifice on the Cross was for Propitiation of the Sins of the Whole World — The Covenant of Holy Eucharist

In blood offering, the life of the victim of the sacrifice is substituted by blood shed on behalf of the offender's life, and accepted as appeasement instead of exacting the life of the offender. In the sacrament of the Holy Eucharist i.e. Holy Qurbana, the most precious Holy Body and Blood together offered, makes it meaningful as a living sacrifice. Thus in every

Holy Qurbana the living Holy Body and Blood of Christ, the God incarnate as the most perfect Son of Man, representing the whole humanity, is offered as supremely acceptable living sacrifice for propitiation of the sins of all the world. Therefore he is in all power and glory at the right hand of God the Father, pleading for the redemption of all humanity. He abides in his believers who partake the Holy Eucharist and they in him. They will be redeemed and accepted in Sonship with Christ before God the Heavenly Father. This is explained by St. Peter and St. Paul the apostles as prophesised by the royal prophet David as follows: "Christ himself carried our sins in his body to the cross, so that we might die to sin and live for righteousness. It is by his wounds that we have been healed."(I Pet. 2:24). It has also opened up the way to the presence of God the Father. Those who believe in him will be justified by their faith and be able to enter the presence of God sanctified and spiritually strong. There is no redeeming act possible for anyone in the Life After Death to count for justification. "But the person who depends on his faith, not on his deeds, and who believes in the God who declares the guilty to be innocent, it is his faith that God takes into account in order to put him right with himself. This is what David meant when he spoke of the happiness of the person whom God accepts as righteous, apart from anything that person does:

Happy are those whose
Wrongs are forgiven,
Whose sins are pardoned!
Happy is the person whose
Sins the Lord will not keep
Account of.

— (Psal. 32: 1-2) & (Rom. 4: 5-8).

Preparation to Enter the Life After Death as Truly Faithful and Intercessory Prayer for Justification by Faith

While we learn about the high privilege of receiving justification by faith as a free gift, we should understand that it is because of the grace bestowed through the sacrifice of Christ on the cross. This knowledge should keep us in the awareness to live in utter faithfulness to God while in this world. True faith should completely rule over us in our daily life and shine through good deeds. The resultant victorious life that aims at perfection becomes guided by divine love. Only if our life is guided like this it would be possible to get in abundance the grace of justification in the Life After Death. By virtue of such abundance of grace only it would be possible to escape from Satan's false claim over our souls alleging as having carried out evil deeds as his servants. By virtue of faith vibrant with true aspiration to live for Christ, the human souls will overcome all such false claims and will become worthy of attaining solace in the bosom of Abraham the father of all the faithful (Paradise). It is in this life in Paradise that souls grow to the perfection required to enter the glorious life in Heaven. The redeeming gift of grace acquired in Paradise through justification by faith would be much greater than the grace of justification by deeds in earthly life; because, in the divine spiritual transparency (I Cor. 13:12) of Paradise the soul would be made ready by self-examination, repentance, worship, intercessory prayers and sanctified for life in Heaven. Adding to the grace received by one's own faith, the grace by the intercessory prayers of others also would enhance the grace of justification by faith for Salvation.

Therefore it is necessary that we in the earthly life should pray in intercession and in the Holy Qurbana before God for those who are departed to Life After Death. This is a filial duty justified according to the Holy Word, especially true of our parents who gave us birth, took all pains to tend us from infancy to become children of God, made us happy in every way and departed from this world. But not praying for them in intercession to God through Christ for granting them the spiritual grace of justification by faith to enter into the solace of Heaven is an unpardonable ingratitude on our part. To say that they will get only according to their deeds and no need of praying for them is sheer ignorance if not callous ingratitude.

Following the Apostolic exhortation "Pray without ceasing" (I Thess. 5:17) we should join in the great intercession of our Lord Jesus Christ before God the Father to offer intercessory prayer for our dear departed ones. It can be done while we worship God or in the solemn moments of private prayers or devotions. We should pray for all the departed souls in our memory. Everyone should be remembered individually in intercession. We should pray even for those who might have had some dislike towards us or have done any evil to us, completely forgiving all trespasses against us. *The great secret of the graceful act of forgiving unconditionally in every detail of the trespasses against us is the hope that it would be in the same measure that God will forgive our trespasses against others. We can forgive only if we have divine love in us*. By forgiving, we are growing towards godliness, because while it is human to err it is godly to forgive. Such forgiving and praying for the ultimate happiness of others in Heaven, would be spiritually perceived by the departed souls owing to their special spiritual ability of perception in the high transparency of the spiritual world. Therefore, in response they will be prompted by divine love to pray for us also. Forgiving fully is the proof of the fullness of love. Thus the love-prompted forgiving spirit that surely invokes divine grace in intercessory prayers from both sides is the prelude to enter the life in Heaven, the abode of divine love and happiness. This is the forgiving spirit of love divine that surpasses all limits to exert its graceful influence in Paradise or Hades too, where the souls, as members of the Church Expectant, get sanctified and made worthy of Heavenly abode. There is no entry for hatred in Heaven. All love and forgiveness is the hope for Salvation. The Holy Spirit of God gives inspiration for this spiritual exercise of divine love to prepare human souls for Salvation. "And be ye kind to one another, tenderhearted, forgiving one another, even as God for Christ's sake hath forgiven you" (Eph. 4:32). "Brethren, if a man be overtaken in a fault, ye which are spiritual, restore such a one in the spirit of meekness; considering thyself, lest thou also be tempted" (Gal 6:1). *Full love forgives fully. Forgiveness is the result of abounding love and that is the solace of Heaven, in the Glorious Life After Death.* Hatred is the result of absence of love and that is the unquenchable fire of Hell. Either of these begins in earthly life invoking the decree of fate in eternity on the Day of Last Judgement.

We should necessarily pray even for those who are known for very unrighteous life. It is in perfect acquiescence with the Spirit of Christ who "died for sins . . . on behalf of sinners" (I Peter 3:18). *". . . . it was while we were still sinners that Christ died for us!"* (Rom 5:8). *"We were God's enemies, but he made us his friends through the death of his Son"* (Rom 5:10). *Also it is the highest service of love in perfect keeping with the new commandment of Christ "Love one another"* (John 13:34), *which has no discrimination between righteous and unrighteous. Intercessory prayer is such a powerful spiritual act that it can work miracles on human souls irrespective of their existence in this life or Life After Death. "This hope does not disappoint us, for God has poured out his love into our hearts by means of the Holy Spirit who is God's gift to us"* (Rom 5:5).

For the departed souls, wherever they are, in Paradise or Hades, the varied refining experiences in the circumstances conducive to self examination and for strengthening them in true faith, our intercessory prayers would be of immense spiritual benefit to them, of course, according to their spiritual status to respond to such refining influences. The departed souls which receive redeeming grace like this, because they are in a spiritual existence and are endowed with super-sensitivity in perception, would be able to understand our love-prompted intercessory prayers for them and be grateful for that. In future when we meet in eternity this would be gratefully remembered by them as a matter of utmost Heavenly joy.

Anywhere, at any time of our life in this world intercessory prayer like this may be offered quite beneficially invoking the grace of justification by faith on the souls of our beloved departed ones. Thus it would be possible to live very fruitfully in this world and continue in the Life After Death in eternity in very endearing communion with other departed souls. Regarding the authenticity of offering intercessory prayers for the departed souls, that pave the way for such a loving spiritual communion, consummated through the Eucharistic Covenant of the Holy Qurbana, clear details can been seen from the explanations given hereunder supported by several quotations from the Holy Bible.

Ordinances of the Old Testament to Remember the Departed Fathers in Sacrificial Offerings

The instructions given by God for making the vestments of the priests, who are to perform the sacrifices for remission of sins of the living and the departed, are very meaningful. God's commands were: "And thou shalt take two onyx stones and engrave on them the names of the children of Israel: Six of their names on one stone and the other six names of the rest on the other stone, according to their birth" (Exodus 28:9, 10). "And Aaron shall bear the names of the children of Israel in the breast plate of judgement upon his heart, when he goeth in unto the holy place, for a memorial before the Lord continually" (Exodus 28:29). The engraving of names of all the tribal fathers of Israel on the spectoral is undoubtedly to remember them in the priestly intercessory prayers offered with the propitiating sacrifices.

In the Jewish Religious Faith

Among the ordinary Jewish believers there was the faith that the Lord shall not let off his kindness to the quick and the dead. This is clear from the fact of belief that Naomi tells her daughter-in-law Ruth, elated at the politeness of Boaz. "Blessed be he of the Lord who hath not let off his kindness to the living and to the dead" (Ruth 2:20). This is recorded in the Holy Word by God's will so that we may also have the same faith.

From the History of Maccabees

Between 168-165 BC, during the Maccabian war many Jewish soldiers were killed. During the interment of these soldiers it was found that small images in gold were hidden by them in their clothes before they were killed. These were images worshipped by people in Jamnia and looted from the battle field. Therefore it was forbidden by law for Jews to wear it. "Every one then knew why these men had been killed. So they praised the ways of the Lord, the just judge, who reveals what is hidden, and they begged him that their sin might be completely blotted out" (II Maccabees 12:41, 42).

See what their illustrious leader Judas has done: He told them to keep away from sin, because they had seen for themselves what had happened to those men who had sinned. "He also took up a collection from all his men totaling about four pounds of silver and sent it to Jerusalem to provide for a sin offering."

"Judas did this noble thing because he believed in the resurrection of the dead" (II Mac. 12:43). "If he had not believed that the dead would be raised, it would have been foolish and useless to pray for them" (Mac 12:44). "In his firm and devout conviction that all of God's faithful people would receive a wonderful reward, Judas made provision for a sin offering to set free from their sin those who had died" (II Mac. 12:45).

Christ's sacrifice on the cross is the fulfilment of the sin offerings as ordained by God and followed in the Jewish religious tradition. That being the offering for propitiation of the sins of the departed souls, it is just and appropriate that we should pray through the merit of that offering as an act of love for our departed ones.

St. Paul Prayed for the Departed Friend

In the II Epistle of St. Paul to Timothy, he recollects with gratitude the loving concern the deceased Onesiphorus had shown to him while he was languishing in the prison in Rome. St. Paul gratefully acknowledges to the family of Onesiphorus, how immediately on arrival at Rome he searched and found him in prison, and cheered him up, visiting several times. St. Paul prays for the family as seen in Ch. 1:16 "May the Lord show mercy to the family of Onesiphorus." This was St. Paul's intercessory prayer for the family of Onesiphorus.

Futher, St. Paul's intercessory payer for the departed soul of Onesiphorus is seen in Ch. 1:18 — "May the Lord grant him his mercy on that Day." This, no doubt, was the intercessory prayer of the Apostle that God may be merciful to the departed soul of Onesiphorus. That Day evidently means the Day of Last Judgement. This also clarifies the fact that till the day of Last Judgement is the period of mercy and God will hear intercessory prayer for mercy on departed souls even in the Life After Death, till the Day of Last Judgement.

Prayer for the family of Onesiphorus can be seen in the 16th verse and prayer for Onesiphorus in the 18th verse. Therefore it can be surely believed that the first intercessory prayer is for those living in this world and the second is for the departed soul. That prayer being a spiritual exercise is effective both for the living and the departed alike is very clear from the above.

The necessity and effectiveness of intercession explained in the foregoing paragraphs are confirmed by this instance of intercession by St. Paul the Apostle.

Hints about Remission of Sins even after Death in Christ's Teachings

For propitiation of sins possibly committed while in this earthly life, there are self-examination, contrition, prayers, confession, Holy Qurbana and such sacramental means. But what about the propitiation for a soul that left this world through death and continues beyond time and space? Some people say that the soul will not get remission of sins in the Life After Death even by offering prayers for that. They try their best to mislead even the faithful by quoting a portion of a verse from the Holy Bible and distorting the real sense in it, as already referred on page 106, i.e. "for all of us must appear before Christ, to be judged by him. Each will receive what he deserves, according to what he has done, good or bad in his bodily life" (II Cor. 5:10). At the same time non-Christians, nay even rustic tribals too perform certain solemnities, sacrifices, appeasing ceremonies and prayers for sanctification of the souls of their beloved departed and derive spiritual satisfaction. What some Christians say and teach is that after death there is no possibility to get remission of sins committed by human weakness in worldly life, for which it was not possible to obtain pardon before death, is in heretic contradiction to what Christ himself has assertively proclaimed.

Christ says: "Wherefore I say unto you, all manner of sin and blasphemy shall be forgiven unto men; but the blasphemy against the Holy Ghost shall not be forgiven unto men. And *whosoever speaketh a word against the Son of Man, it shall be forgiven him: but whosoever speaketh against the Holy Ghost, it shall not be forgiven him, neither in this world, neither in the world to come."* (Matt. 12:31, 32).

How clearly it can be understood from this, that there is possibility of remission of sins in the world to come, i.e. in the world in which the soul continues to live in eternity. But, for the sin of blasphemy against the Holy Ghost only there will not be remission even in the eternal life. It is a state of existence in pride and self-justification devoid of any repentance and so impossible to get any remission of sins, and deserving eternal condemnation with Satan. Anyone should hearken unto this warning and be in constant vigilance to avoid falling into this unremittable condemnation.

How undoubtably it is stated here by our Lord that excepting for blasphemy against Holy Ghost, there is possibility of remission of all other sins in this world as well as in the other world till the Day of the Last Judgement.

From the scripture portions quoted above, it is clear that there is possibility of remission of sins for human souls even in the Life After Death, by means of their true faith, contrition, supplication and intercessory prayers of others in unison with the great intercession of Christ before God the Father, till the day of Last Judgement. Therefore our departed ones, even though they may be sinners, our intercessory prayers, offerings and Holy Qurbana the propitiating sacrifice, adorations and charities on their behalf, will be effective for the remission of their sins, strengthening and sanctification of their souls. It is the hope and assurance of the justification by true faith in the redeeming grace of our Lord Jesus Christ.

(D) COMMUNION WITH GOD IN THE EARTHLY LIFE CONTINUES IN THE AFTER-DEATH LIFE ALSO AS A PROFOUND ECSTASY

The Church which Keeps Vigil for the Bridegroom in the Earthly Life as in the Life After Death

King Solomon, who is considered to have been the wisest among the wise, has written a book called "Solomon's Songs" qualified as the "Song of Songs." In that he has compared the divine love of Christ towards the Church and in turn the divine love the Church shows towards Christ, as the love between the bridegroom and bride. A few examples are given hereunder:

"Draw me, we will run after thee: the king hath brought me into his chambers we will be glad and rejoice in thee, we will remember thy love more than wine: the upright love thee" (S.S 1:4). This is the experience of the faithful getting away from the earthly life to the promised abode. Attracted and pulled by the love of Christ, the bride (Church) is anxious to sort out the estranged life in the far-off life and hasten to join the royal bridegroom in his abode.

"My beloved spake, and said unto me, Rise up, my love, my fair one, and come away." "For, lo, the winter is past, the rain is over and gone" (S.S 2:10,11). The cold days of the earthly life are over. Christ the redeemer is calling the children of the Church to the glowing warmth of the Glorious Life After Death with him.

"Thou art all fair, my love, there is no spot in thee" (S.S 4:7). God created Adam as a person of charm and beauty. Though it was defiled by sin, Christ redeemed the human soul to the same celestial beauty and perfection. This regaining of spiritual beauty is only possible by the grace of justification granted by the Lord.

"Behold thou art fair my love . . . behold thou art fair . . . my beloved, yea, pleasant: . . ." (S.S 1:15, 16) — a view of the ecstasy of mutual love between Christ the bridegroom and Church the bride.

We have nothing except what we have received from God. But God the giver of everything knows the beauty and elegance of Heavenly glories with which man is adorned. Without leaving such a perfectly delightful creation to be destroyed by Satan, God took incarnation as human. Giving his own life blood as Son of Man he has offered himself as sacrifice in propitiation for the sin of the world to redeem everyone who believes in him, from the curse of sin to spiritual beauty and perfection. If we understand and live with full faith in him in this earthly life, even in the Life After Death we would be still closely attached to him. Therefore King Solomon, who visualises the depth of love in the union of the Messiah and the Church, is describing this as the communion between the bride and the bridegroom in his Song of Songs with a very appreciable elegance.

"I sleep but my heart waketh: it is the voice of my beloved that knocketh, saying, Open to me, my sister, my love, my dove, my undefiled. . . . " (S.S. 5:2). Whether in the slumber of the physical body or in the repose of the Life After Death, the soul that has deep consciousness about the love of God will always be alert to hear the loving voice in the call of Christ the saviour. Though in the spiritual state the heart will be alert to hear the voice of Christ because even in the tumult of earthly life it preserved Christ's love as the lively force that outlives death as the hope in eternity. This is in comparison with the bride who harkens unto the voice of the beloved Lord of her heart and opens the door to receive him.

Solomon's vision about the Church as the bride of Christ awaiting the knock of the beloved at the door, revealing the deep and hearty love of Christ, so beautifully described, offers great love-prompted hope to the believers. From all these it is clear that human souls which are so lively in the Life After Death are growing in the love of God by communion with him and are progressing towards perfection in eternity.

Communion with God in the Secret Garden of the Soul Continuing even in the Life After Death

God is the supreme spirit, and the inner thirst of a human soul to have spiritual communion with him is quite natural. But much deeper than that is the yearning of God to commune with man who is created in his own image. If we have not understood this divine secret, there is nothing more unfortunate than that. If children who approach father only to get some favour granted, ignore him at other times, how poor is that father and children relationship?

God knows even the slightest sigh of the human soul. God's attention is there always for any call of the soul. This is an amazing truth. But we do not realise this properly. Many are the experiences of our fathers of the past who have observed the holy moments of secret prayer as the unfailing priority of their daily life in divine communion with God. Before they enter into the daily routine of earthly life or set apart some time from all mundane matters, and turn their heart desiring communion with God, lo, He would already be there in the secret garden of the soul, ready for the communion. David who had the favour of God's heart, realizing this truth, says "*When thou saidst "Seek ye my face," my heart said unto thee, "Thy face, Lord, I will seek"* (Psal. 27:8). In response, offering himself for communion he says in prayer: "Hide not thy face far from me; put not thy servant away in anger: thou hast been my help, leave me not, neither forsake me, O God of my Salvation" (Psal. 27:9). ". . . *I remember thee upon my bed and meditate on thee in the night watches"* (Psal. 63:6).

Solitary Devotion of Nathaniel

Until Philipose introduced Nathaniel to Jesus they have never seen each other bodily. *"Nathaniel saith unto him, whence knowest thou me?" Jesus answered and said unto him, "Before that Philip called thee, when thou wast under the fig tree, I saw thee"* (John 1:48). *Then, Nathaniel who had the daily habit of sitting under the thick shade of a fig tree, in the very early morning, without anybody's knowledge and seeking the face of God in meditation, immediately realised that Jesus is the Son of God who is omnipresent and is able to understand the secret of any soul from anywhere and at any time.*

Secret Prayer of Daniel in the Upper Room

Daniel had the routine of praying on his knees in his room privately before God's presence, three times a day (Dan. 6:10). What was the result? *The arch angel Gabriel appeared and explained: "At the beginning of thy supplication, the commandment came forth and I am come to shew thee; for thou art greatly beloved;* therefore understand the matter, and consider the vision" (Dan 9:23).

If those who regularly find time amongst many mundane business affairs to wait for the grace and favours from God, how much more could human souls in Life After Death beyond interferences and worldly influences, find concentration and joy of communion with God?

This is a matter of great hope in Life After Death. In the earthly life too what decides the future of the soul is the virtue earned by pleasing God by regular heart-felt communion and worship, as could be seen from the above. This habit of worship is an asset to make the Life After Death quite happy and glorious for the soul.

7

Second Coming of the Lord Jesus Christ, Resurrection of the Dead and the Final Judgement

THE three great events mentioned above mutually related to each other are going to happen in future. From the hints provided about them in the Holy Bible we have to understand that their occurrence may be at some time in the future. We can only imagine that each of these events that mark the culmination of ages, would be utmost wonderful and awe-inspiring to the uttermost. To get any hint on the details we have to depend only upon the Holy Bible. Of course, they would be the experiences of those who have departed to eternity from this world from its very beginning as well as those who are alive now and die before those events. Therefore it is appropriate to discuss about such matters which can decisively influence the after-death conditions of human souls.

Second Coming of the Lord Jesus Christ

On the 40th day of the Resurrection of Jesus Christ he ascended to Heaven as his disciples were looking on. ". . . He was taken up and a cloud received him out of their sight. And while they looked steadfastly toward Heaven as he went up, two men stood by them in white apparel, who also said, "Ye men of Galilee, why stand ye gazing up into Heaven? This same Jesus which is taken up from you into Heaven, shall come in like manner as ye have seen him go into Heaven" (Acts. 1:9-11). Oh, what a heartening promise! It is not surprising if they anticipated that this coming back may happen the very next day.

Like the Lord's Resurrection from the grave, his ascension to Heaven also was the most wonderful and unparalleled event in the entire world history. And there is no doubt that the promise which the messengers of the Lord so firmly gave also would happen in the history of the world. Christ who disappeared in the cloud and ascended to Heaven will come again to the world appearing in cloud in the same way. It is a truth which we believe and acknowledge every day in our worship.

It is not for us to know as to the times or season when it is going to happen, which God the Father has put in his own power (Acts 1:7). But we look towards it with true faith and hope. However, it is our duty to be well aware of it and be prepared, whether we will be in this world or in the next world.

When Jesus Christ was living in this world as a man, he spoke about his second coming as requested by his disciples. It is given in the Gospel of St. Matthew "For as the lightning cometh out of the East, and shineth even up to the West; so shall also the coming of the Son of Man be" (Matt. 24:27). "*And then shall appear the sign of the Son of Man in Heaven; and then shall all the tribes of the earth mourn and they shall see the Son of Man coming in the clouds of Heaven with power and great glory. And he shall send his angels with a great sound of a trumpet, and they shall gather together his elect from the four winds, from one end of the Heaven and the other*" (Mat 24:30, 31). It is gathering together of the departed that happens in the resurrection. Jesus Christ has revealed the prophesy about this important event to his disciples on many occasions:

"Jesus saith unto him. Thou hast said: nevertheless I say unto you, hereafter shall ye see the Son of Man sitting on the right hand of power and coming in the clouds of Heaven" (Mat 26:64).

"And then shall they see the Son of Man coming in the clouds with great power and glory. And then shall he send his angels and shall gather together his elect from the four winds, from the uttermost part of the earth to the uttermost part of Heaven" (Mark 13:26, 27).

"Watch ye therefore: for ye know not when the master of the house cometh, at even or at midnight or at the cockcrowing or in the morning: Lest coming suddenly he find you sleeping" (Mark 13:35, 36).

"And Jesus said, I am and ye shall see the Son of Man sitting on the right hand of power and coming in the clouds of Heaven" (Mark 14:62).

"Men's hearts failing them for fear, and for looking after those things which are coming on the earth; for the powers of Heaven shall be shaken. And then shall they see Son of Man coming in a cloud with power and great glory. And when these things begin to come to pass, then look up and lift your heads, your redemption draweth nigh" (Luk. 21: 26-28).

St. Paul explains about this event in his epistle like this:

"But every man in his own order: Christ the first fruits; afterward they that are Christ's at his coming. Then cometh the end, when he shall have delivered up the Kingdom to God, even the Father; when he shall have put down all rule and all authority and power" (I Cor 15: 23, 24).

"For what is our hope or joy or crown of rejoicing? Are not even ye in the presence of our Lord Jesus Christ at his coming? For ye are our Glory and joy" (I Thess. 2:19,20).

"To the end he may stablish your hearts unblameable in holiness before God, even our Father, at the coming of our Lord Jesus Christ with all his saints" (I Thess. 3:13).

"For the Lord himself shall descend from Heaven with a shout, with a voice of the archangel and with the trump of God: and the dead in Christ shall rise first" (I Thess. 4:16).

"Be patient therefore, brethren, unto the coming of the Lord" (James 5:7).

"And now little children, abide in him; that when he shall appear, we may have confidence and not be ashamed before him at his coming" (I John 2:28).

In the Revelations of St. John it is written: "And I, John saw the holy city, New Jerusalem, coming down from God out of Heaven, prepared as a bride adorned for her husband. And I heard a great voice out of Heaven saying, "Behold the tabernacle of God is with men and he will dwell with them and they shall be his people and God himself shall be with them and be their God. And God shall wipe away all tears from their eyes and there shall be no more death, neither sorrow, nor crying, neither shall there be any more pain: for the former things are passed away." And he that sat upon the throne said, Behold I make all things new. . . ." (Rev. 21:2-5).

It is hinted in all the foregoing words that the Church Expectant that has departed from the earthly life and are hid with Christ in God (Colos. 3:3) *also would come with him in his second coming from Heaven to earth.*

Resurrection of the Dead — A Great Event to Precede the Day of Last Judgement

The souls of the faithful who are hid with Christ in Paradise are there as spiritual beings. They adore God and are waiting for the Last Judgement expecting from God the grant of the reward they deserve for the glorious virtues they have earned while in the earthly life. ". . . The Lord shall judge his people" (Heb. 10:30). Before that, as said in the previous chapter, ". . . there shall be a resurrection of the dead both of the just and unjust" (Acts 24:15).

The Glorious Hope of the Resurrection

"Thou turnest men to destruction; and sayest "Return ye children of men" (Psal. 90: 3).

Though by death the physical human body may perish and join dust to dust, on the day of resurrection every human soul will get its own physical body glorified, maintaining its identity of the person. This is dealt with in detail in the vision which the prophet Ezekiel had. Its relevant portions are as hereunder: (Ezekiel 37:1-14).

"The hand of the Lord was upon me and carried me out in the spirit of the Lord and set me down in the midst of the valley which was full of bones. And caused me to pass by them round about: and behold, there were many in the open valley; and lo they were very dry. And he said unto me, Son of man, can these bones live? And I answered, O Lord God thou knowest. Again he said unto me, Prophesy upon these bones and say unto them, O ye dry bones, hear the Word of the Lord. Thus Sayeth the Lord God unto these bones; Behold, I will cause breath to enter into you and ye shall live. And I will lay sinews upon you and will bring up flesh upon you, and cover you with skin, and put breath in you and ye shall live; and ye shall know that I am Lord. So I prophesied as I was commanded: and as I prophesied there was a noise, and behold a shaking and the bones came together, bone to his bone. And when I beheld, lo, the sinews and the flesh came up upon them and the skin covered them above: but there was no breath in them. Then said he unto me, prophesy unto the wind, Prophesy Son of man and say unto the wind, Thus saith the Lord God; Come from the four winds, O breath, and breathe upon these slain, that they may live. So I prophesied as he commanded me, and the breath came into them and they lived and stood up on their feet, an exceeding great army. Then he said unto me, Son of man, these bones are the whole house of Israel: behold they say, Our bones are dried and our hope is lost: we are cut off from our parts. Therefore prophesy and say unto them, Thus saith the Lord God; Behold, O my people, I will open your graves, and cause you come up out of your graves, and bring you unto the land of Israel. And ye shall know that I am the Lord, when I opened your graves, O my people and brought you out of your graves. And shall put my spirit in you and ye shall live. . ." (Ezek. 37:1-14). Resurrection of the dead is the hope in the Life After Death.

In this prophesy of Ezekiel cited above, because it is said that "these bones are the whole house of Israel," some people say that it is related to the people of Israel only and not to the resurrection of all mankind. That is not correct, because resurrection is not only for the people of Israel. In the thoughts of the Israelite prophet the interest of his own people was foremost and it is quite natural. Though their hope was dim by death he was specifically mentioning to them about resurrection, exhorting and confirming them in the hope of redemption to a new life of solace in eternity. This exhortation is not confined to any political or sectarian limits. In the great plan of God for Salvation of mankind which is beyond the conception of man, to bring communal or such short-sighted interpretations would be detracting from God's ways. What is declared as given by God to his people, like the Ten Commandments, is not for any one section of people, but for the entire world for all times. The loving salutation "O my people" is the expression of God's endearing divine love towards all mankind whom he created in his own image. As stated above all mankind, good as well as evil, will resurrect, to stand before God to be judged.

Resurrecting Body would be Glorified and Individually Identifiable

It is hinted in the above mentioned prophesy that before the Last Judgement of all, every one will be resurrected in a glorified body in such a manner as each one person can be clearly identified. The mortal remains in the grave, however degenerated, would be given perfection and life in resurrection, as could be seen from the Gospels. "Marvel not at this: for the hour is coming, in which all that are in the graves shall hear his voice. And shall come forth; they that have done good, unto resurrection of life; and they that have done evil, unto the resurrection of damnation" (John 5:28, 29).

In Resurrection it is Rising up Like Angels

The Sadducees who deny that there is any resurrection asked Jesus Christ questioning about the state of married life in the physical world and the state of life after resurrection. The answer given by the Lord is clear about the state of life that continues after death. "And Jesus answering said unto them, The children of this world marry and are given in marriage; But they which shall be accounted worthy to obtain that world and the resurrection from the dead, neither marry, nor are given in marriage. Neither can they die any more; for they are equal unto the angels; and are the children of God, being the children of the resurrection (Luk. 20:34-36). There is nothing like sex or sexual difference in the resurrected body.

Transformation of those Alive at the Time of the Lord's Second Coming

As the second coming of the Lord is going to happen at any time in the future of human history, what will happen to those who would be alive at that time, is clearly said by St. Paul the Apostle: "Now this I say brethren, that flesh and blood cannot inherit the kingdom of God; neither doth corruption inherit incorruption. Behold, I shew you a mystery; we shall not all sleep, but we shall all be changed. In a moment, in the twinkling of an eye, at the last trump; for the trumpet shall sound and the dead shall be raised incorruptible and we shall be changed. For this corruptible must put on incorruption and this mortal must put on immortality. So when this corruptible shall have put on incorruption and this mortal shall have put on immortality, then shall be brought to pass the saying that is written, Death is swallowed up in victory. Oh death, where is thy sting, Oh grave, where is thy victory?. . ." (I Cor. 15: 50-55).

The continuation of this event is described by St. Paul in his 1st Epistle to Thessalonians: "For the Lord himself shall descend from Heaven with a shout, with the voice of the archangel and with the trumpet of God: and the dead in Christ shall rise first. Then we which are alive and remain shall be caught up together with them in the clouds, to meet the Lord in the air: and so shall we ever be with the Lord" (I Thess. 4:16-17).

The Body Transformed is Glorified

In the great event of giving life to the departed and raising them up in resurrection from the grave, explained in the prophesy of the prophet Ezekiel, what is seen in corruption is raised in incorruption; what is seen in dishonour is raised in glory, what is seen as a temporal body is raised as spiritual body. St. Paul's description is also identical; "So also is the resurrection of the dead. It is sown in corruption; it is raised in incorruption: It is sown in dishonour; it is raised in glory: It is sown in weakness; it is raised in power: It is sown a natural body; it is raised a spiritual body. There is a natural body and there is a spiritual body" (I Cor. 15:42-44).

The resurrected uncorrupt body would be a spiritual body like that of angels bearing the Heavenly image worthy to inherit the kingdom of God. This is exactly as stated in the Epistle of St. Paul: "And as we have borne the image of the earthy, we shall also bear the image of the Heavenly" (I Cor. 15:49).

How this Happens?

St. Paul explains this secret by an example: "Someone will ask, "How can the dead be raised to life? What kind of body will they have?" You fool! When you plant a seed in the ground, it does not sprout to life unless it dies. And what you plant is a bare seed, perhaps a grain of wheat or some other grain, not the full bodied plant that will later grow up. God provides that seed with the body he wishes; he gives each seed its own proper body" (I Cor. 15:35-38). "Seed dies in order to give birth to a seedling."*

In Resurrection the Soul Becomes Identified to Christ the First Fruit

"But now is Christ risen from the dead, and become the first fruits of them that slept. For since by man came death, by man came also the resurrection of the dead. For as in Adam all die, even so in Christ shall all be made alive. But every man in his own order: Christ the first fruits; afterward they

---

* Para 2, Page 21 of "*Introduction to The Bhagavad Gītā*" by Swami Chidbhavānanda.

that are Christ's at his coming. Then cometh the end, when he shall have delivered up the kingdom to God, even the Father; when he shall have put down all rule and all authority and power" (I Cor. 15:20-24).

Adam the First Man of the Earth is Garmented in the Image of the Heavenly Second Adam (Christ)

"And so it is written, The first man Adam was made a living soul; the last Adam was made a quickening spirit. Howbeit that was not first which is spiritual, but that which is natural; and afterward that which is spiritual. The first man of the earth, earthy: the second man is the Lord from Heaven. As is the earthy, such are they also that are earthy: and as is the Heavenly, such are they also that are Heavenly. And as we have borne the image of the earthy we shall also bear the image of the Heavenly" (I Cor. 15:45-49).

Transformation to the Image of the Heavenly One

Jesus Christ said: "For in the resurrection they neither marry, nor are given in marriage, but are as the angels of God in Heaven" (Mat 22:30). Body of the angels is Heavenly and not temporal earthly body. The body that humans get in resurrection after death is a Heavenly body as that of angels. There are hints in the Bible that angels have got personally identifying individual names. Therefore it is sure that the glorified human body we get in resurrection also would be having enough clarity of features for individual identity as we already had in this world. Especially the name sealed in the Holy Baptism would be relevant even in the Life After Death. Even though all may not be having a Baptismal Name, every one would be having an identifying name in this world. Similarly in the spiritual world of eternity also every human soul would be personally identifiable. It is because of identifying everyone on resurrection that everyone is getting the individually deserving reward in the Final Judgement on his deeds in earthly life.

Not only those who were dead and resurrecting that are getting this type of Heavenly body, those who are alive at the second coming would also be transforming like that in the twinkling of any eye. It is because they are transforming into Heavenly spiritual body, along with those resurrecting into Heavenly body (which is not subject to gravitational force of the earth) they get the ability to be caught up together with them in the clouds to receive the Lord in the sky (See I Thess. 4:16-17).

The Heavenly Lord Incarnated as Earthly Man to Transform the Earthly Man as Heavenly

Though Adam was formed out of the dust of the ground by God, he was a creation in the image of God. In order to expiate the curse brought about by sin, the Son of God himself came incarnated as the Son of Man, taken up the sins of all humanity on himself and died on the cross on behalf of man as propitiation, and resurrected on the third day. That sinless Heavenly Jesus Christ the Son of Man bequeathed through him the sonship as the legacy of acceptance for earthly Adam and his descendants before God the Father. Since the Son of God incarnate as Son of Man, died and resurrected the way is opened for humans to the merit of Gods sonship. "In whom we have redemption through his blood, the forgiveness of sins, according to the riches of his grace" (Eph. 1:7). This is the great miracle that happens in human life that gloriously enters eternity through death.

Specialties of the Heavenly Body

The Lord Jesus Christ, who incarnated as a human was a perfect man and at the same time entirely God so as to accomplish the redemption of Adam and his descendants to the Sonship of God the Father. The Heavenly Lord lived on this earth as an ordinary man; living in a mortal human body for 33 years requiring for his perfectly human body, food, rest etc. as any other human being. He had the congenital perfection of ordinary human beings and was representing humanity in all respects except sin. Still in his earthly lifetime, only on very rare occasions he allowed the exuberance of his divinity to shine out. Even Satan who tempted him to jump from the pinnacle of the temple was very well aware of his divinity and said that angels would bear him up in their hands. Yet he was not amenable to such temptations for propagating his ministry resorting to display of his divinity and performing miracles of that sort.

However, water made wine was his first recorded miracle in which his divinity was manifested. Feeding many thousands with five loaves of bread and proceeding quickly from mountain top to his disciples out at sea in peril during the night and appearing to them by walking over water near their boat, are all signs which reveal his divinity.

That perfect representation of humanity as he was, he died on the Calvary cross, commending his spirit into the hands of God the Father, and his human body which was dead and buried in a tomb, when resurrected on the third day, became glorified as Heavenly body. We can remember only with utmost love and devotion our saviour Jesus Christ who revealed to us the uniqueness of the glorified body through the events that followed the resurrection. As we have been adorned in the image of one who created us out of dust in the physical life, in the Life After Death in resurrection also we would be gloriously adorned in the image of the Heavenly Lord. Let us be hopeful for that glorious blessing.

How immaculate and grand was the glorified Heavenly body of the resurrected Lord Jesus Christ, is evident from the many events after the resurrection, as recorded in the Holy Bible. After the Lord's resurrection: "Then the same day at evening, being the first day of the week, when the doors were shut, where the disciples were assembled for fear of the Jews, came Jesus and stood in the midst, and saith unto them, Peace be unto you. And when he had so said, he showed unto them his hands and his side. Then were the disciples glad, when they saw the Lord" (John 20:19, 20).

The same day when Cleopas and his friend were walking on their way from Jerusalem to a village called Emmaus, Jesus appeared to them as a casual pedestrian, drew near and walked with them (But their eyes were hidden that they should not know him). It was with the resurrected body that he walked with them expounding the things of the holy words and went to their home accepting their invitation to stay with them for the night. "And it came to pass, as he sat at meal with them, he took bread, and blessed it and broke and gave to them. And their eyes were opened and they knew him and he vanished out of their sight" (Luk. 24:30, 31).

Again after eight days when the disciples were in a room the disciple Thomas also was there. Even when the door was closed Jesus came in their midst and said "Peace be to you." Then, saith he unto Thomas, "Reach hither your finger and behold my hands; and reach hither thy hand, and thrust it into my side: and be not faithless, but believing" (John 20:27).

Even though the body was a glorified Heavenly body, that could easily enter into a closed room, appear, talk and disappear, it was consistent to be sensed by touch by Thomas with his fingers. It is also noteworthy that at that time the resurrected body of Our Lord was clad in glorious vestments and not in the grave clothes that were left in the Sepulchre. Glorious vestments only can enter with the glorious body, appear and disappear like that, and not the earthly clothes.

Though we live in this world clad in earthly clothes, on our resurrection we are going to get glorified vestments for our glorified Heavenly body. In fulfillment of the Holy Word "And as we have borne the image of the earthy, we shall also bear the image of the Heavenly" (I Cor. 15:49). God being omnipresent will be present everywhere at the same time. But the angels and humans who get glorified body can be present only at one place at one time. The shine and lustre of such vestments would be from the shine and lustre of the Heavenly body granted to us by the Grace of God commensurate with the merit of the loving deeds of righteousness while living in this world. The glorious Prophet Isaiah in his prophesy (54:5) states: " For thy maker is thine husband, the Lord of hosts is his name, and the Redeemer, the Holy one . . . The God. . . ." Further, the redeemed Church personified as the bride continues: (Isiah 61:10) "I will greatly rejoice in the Lord, my soul shall be joyful in my God: for he hath clothed me with the garments of salvation, he hath covered me with the robe of righteousness . . . as a bride adorneth herself with her jewels." What a joy it is to be the bride of the Redeemer in the eternal life in Heaven! Therefore, let us be diligent in loving deeds of righteousness, making best use of our lifetime here to enter the Glorious Life After Death.

8

The Final Judgement

And it is Appointed unto Men Once to Die and then the Judgement (Heb. 9:27)

The Last Judgement is the great event which decides the destiny of all mankind. The awe-inspiring moment in which every one would receive the judgement that decides his final destination, either in Heaven the abode of eternal bliss or in Hell the cursed place of eternal suffering. The Holy Word very definitely states: "We shall all stand before the judgement seat of Christ" (Rom 14:10). The Last Judgement which nobody can escape would be different from any judgements before that. About that Christ has said: "But I say unto you, that every idle word that men shall speak, they shall give account thereof in the day of judgement" (Matt. 12:36).

God's judgements that have come on mankind from the beginning of the world are numerous, as historical happenings. Even at the beginning of the Biblical history, in judgement of the transgression of the early parents in the Garden of Eden, they were banished from there. From then onwards, examples of judgement are numerous, like the one specifically mentioned by St. Stephen about God's judgement on the nation of Pharaoh who kept the Israelites in bondage for 400 years (Acts 7:6). They are continuing as if it is certain that there is a God who is closely observing the deeds of all people. Not only individuals but also communities as well as nations are subjected to judgement and get into troubles and tribulations of punishment and are absolved in due course. But all these are viewed as God's interventions through acts of punishments to discipline humans for turning them to right paths.

But the Last Judgement will be either to cast the offenders into the Hell-fire prepared for Satan and his hosts or else to welcome the faithful to the eternal joy of Heaven. The reward will be according to the merit earned by each soul during its life on earth: ". . . revelation of the righteous judgement of God: who will render to every man according to his deeds" (Rom 2:6) and "justification by faith" (Rom. 3:24, 27, 28). "Being justified freely by his grace through the redemption that is in Christ Jesus" (Rom. 3:24), where is boasting then: It is excluded. By what law? Of works? Nay: but by law of faith." (Rom. 3:27). "Therefore we conclude that a man is justified by faith without the deeds of the law" (Rom. 3:28).

Everything Good or Bad Seen Openly

"Some men's sins are open beforehand, going before to judgement and some men they follow after. Likewise also the good works of some are manifest beforehand; and they that are otherwise cannot be hid" (I Thim. 5:24, 25). It is not possible to hide anything on the Last Judgement day. Those who do not listen to the declaration of the Gospel of Salvation and live riotously denying God, will face the Last Judgement to be sentenced to everlasting doom.

"He will do this when the Lord Jesus appears from Heaven with his mighty angels, with a flaming fire, to punish those who reject God and who do not obey the Good news about our Lord Jesus. They will suffer the punishment of eternal destruction, separated from the presence of the Lord and from his glorious might" (II Thess. 1:7-9).

Faith in Christ as the Covenant of Salvation in the Life After Death Also

But Jesus Christ has very clearly and firmly said that those who hear his words and live a life of love and faith in God, when facing the Last Judgement have no need to be afraid but only to be glad. It is because they are worthy of Salvation and not condemnation. "Verily verily I say unto you, He that heareth my word, and believeth on him that sent me, hath everlasting life, and shall not come into condemnation: but is passed from death unto life" (John 5:24).

By faith one achieves the worthiness and grace for the remission of sins. It is possible for the faithful to be absolved of transgression and to enter Salvation through faith in Christ.

The Creed. The Creed which proclaims the faith in the Holy Trinity, Christ's death on the cross for our Salvation, his burial, resurrection, ascension and the second coming to judge the quick and the dead, is a saving dogmatic tenet which should be perpetually in the mind of a truly faithful person. Especially when one is in the final stages of physical life, about to enter the Life After Death, it is a good practice someone recites the Creed loudly so that the dying person can hear it and meditate on it. This is a very meaningful and essential thing to be done representing the departing person. This noble practice is helpful in exhorting the person entering through death to the Glorious Life After Death with the hope of the grace of eternal deliverance through justification by faith in Christ.

God shall Wipe Away All Tears from their Eyes

The faithful who lead truly devoted life get comfort for all their sorrows and reward for their life of moral excellence on the day of Last Judgement. Because of moral principles followed without surrendering to evil; the miseries and losses suffered during physical life will all be compensated and there would be relief from all sorrows. "God will wipe away all tears from their eyes" (Rev. 7:17). "And God shall wipe away all tears from their eyes, and there shall be no more death, neither sorrow, nor crying, neither shall there be any more pain, for the former things are passed away" (Rev 21:4). The joy we experience as gift of God on the day of Last Judgement will be much more than our wildest expectations. "Therefore judge nothing before time, until the Lord comes, who both will bring to light the hidden things of darkness, and will make manifest the counsels of the hearts: and then shall every man have praise of God" (I Cor. 4:5). "There is therefore now no condemnation to them which are in Christ Jesus, who walk not after the flesh, but after the spirit" (Rom 8:1).

God's Son Became Son of Man to Make Sons of Man God's Sons

It is a very very comforting and hopeful truth that the judge who sits for Final Judgement is the Son of God who gave his own life blood in sacrifice for the remission of our sins and now continually intercedes with God the Father for us. This is a fact which Lord Jesus himself has told: "For the Father judgeth no man, but hath committed all judgement unto the Son: That all men should honour the Son. That all men should honour the Son even as they honour the Father. . ." (John 5:22, 23). "For as the Father has life in himself, so hath he given to the Son to have life in himself; and hath given him authority to execute judgement also, because he is the Son of Man" (John 5:26, 27). "For in that He himself hath suffered being tempted, he is able to succour them that are tempted" (Heb. 2:18). "For we have not a high priest which cannot be touched with the feelings of our infirmities; but was at all points tempted like as we are, yet without sin" (Heb 4:15).

Therefore he will show full sympathy and compassion to the truly devoted people who are afflicted by trials by the world, flesh and Satan, and approach him in contrition. We believe that out of mercy he will redeem them granting them justification by their faith.

The reason and truth for such a belief is expressed by St. Paul the Apostle as in the epistle he wrote to the Romans as follows:-

"5: (14) But from the time of Adam to the time of Moses, death ruled over all mankind, even over those who did not sin in the same way that Adam did when he disobeyed God's command.

"5: (15) Adam was the figure of the one man who was to come. But the two are not the same because God's free gift is not like Adam's sin. It is true that many people died because of the sin of that one man. But God's grace is much greater, and so is his free gift to so many people through the grace of one man Jesus Christ.

"5: (16) And there is a difference between God's gift and the sin of one man. After the one sin, came the judgement of "Guilty"; but after so many sins, comes the undeserved gift of "Not Guilty."

"5: (17) It is true that through the sin of one man death began to rule because of that one man. But how much greater is the result of what was done by the one man, Jesus Christ! All who receive God's abundant grace and are freely put right with him will rule in the life through Christ.

"5: (18) So then, as the one sin condemned all mankind, in the same way the one righteous act sets all mankind free and gives them life.

"5: (19) And just as all people were made sinners as the result of the disobedience of one man, in the same way they will be put right with God as the result of the obedience of the one man" (Rom 5:19)."

Because of Adam the one who disobeyed the command of God by eating the forbidden fruit the curse of spiritual death came upon him and it has been communicated to his descendants who were also put under the shadow of spiritual death. But to redeem the beloved creation of God, the Son of God who incarnated as the Son of Man took on himself the curse of sin and shed his sinless blood on the Calvary cross as propitiating sacrifice for the sins of all mankind. Thus he redeemed mankind from the curse of sin. This is the divine secret of granting the inheritance of eternal life to all who believe in this redeeming sacrifice that is explained in the verses quoted above.

Like this, while facing the Last Judgement in the Life After Death, Jesus Christ is giving to true believers in him the free gift of Salvation inherited in eternal life without condemnation to the damnation of spiritual death. The truth here is, because Christ, born as the Son of Man, by his sacrifice on the cross acquired for mankind the remission of sins. Therefore mankind got entrance before God the Father through Christ by the merit of his Sonship promised to us. "Verily Verily I say unto you, he that heareth my word and believeth on Him that sent me, hath everlasting life and shall not come into condemnation, but is passed from death to life" (John 5:24). The grace of Sonship is the promise offered to believers for Salvation. This grace of Sonship received through Baptism is a blessed divine privilege to be kept up by faith transferred to descendants since this grace bestows the worthiness to receive the verdict for Salvation on Last Judgement day; it has to be very prayerfully kept alive throughout life to be carried over to the Glorious Life After Death. As mentioned above, ". . . but after so many sins comes the undeserved gift of "Not Guilty" (Rom 5:16). Spiritually born again into the true faith, as a new creation, the believer should lead a truly dedicated righteous life to receive this gift for salvation (2 Cor. 5:17). We have to be guided by the Holy Spirit for this. God gives Holy Spirit to those that ask Him. "If ye then, being evil, know how to give good gifts to your children, how much more your Heavenly Father give the Holy Spirit to those that ask Him?" (Luk.11:13).

Dispensation of the Final Judgement

". . . How unsearchable are his judgement and his ways past finding out" (Rom 11:33). The Last Judgement is an event that will happen some time in the future. It is impossible for any one to say anything about it. However, as mentioned in the previous para, the Son of Man, Jesus Christ is given authority to execute the Judgement. During his life on this earth he has given some hints as to how it would be, as could be seen from the Gospels. Since these are very important matters which we may have to face in the Life After Death we have to take necessary preparation for that without wasting any time, even while living in this world. It would be useful to discuss about that in the light of the Holy Bible.

God is Love (I John 4:16)

Everyone will accept that the acts of God incarnated as the Son of Man, done in his public ministry in this world, culminating in his death for the remission of the sins of the world, consummating in his resurrection and ultimately in his ascension into Heaven after giving the promise of his return to take us to his father's house, are all very loving deeds. But it may not be possible for many to believe that the motivating and deciding factor that is going to be manifest in the Last

Judgement also is the same divine love. The simple and beautiful hints regarding this, which we can see in the Bible, will convince us as to how invaluable and adorable is the love that outlives death in the Life After Death making it glorious.

Love-based Life, the Experience of Abiding in God

The Will of God that shines through the Ten Commandments is that we should lead our life in this world in real love for God and men. For those who lead life well established in divine love, will definitely have the experience of God, who is love, abiding in them and they in him. This is a very sacred and transcendent divine relationship. This divine spiritual relationship will bestow great confidence to the human soul before God on the day of Final Judgement. "But whoso keepeth his word, in him, verily is the love of God perfected: hereby know we that we are in him. He that saith he abideth in him, ought himself also so to walk, even as he walked" (I John 2:5, 6). "Let that therefore abide in you, which ye have heard from the beginning. If that which ye have heard from the beginning shall remain in you, ye also shall continue in the Son and in the Father" (I John 2:24). "And now, little children, abide in him, that, when he shall appear, we may have confidence, and not be ashamed before him at his coming" (I John 2:28).

The Attitude we Foster should be the One that Christ Jesus had

How to attain the very high spiritual grace of abiding in God and its manifestation in life is stated in such a simple and beautiful way by St. Paul in his Epistle to Philippines: "Let this mind be in you, which was also in Christ Jesus" (Phili. 2:5). That is, we should live like Christ, absorbing Christ in everything. It means, in whatever situation in which we are, if it were Christ, imagine what would he do, and do like that. Once a central government officer, a true believer who was in service for a long period, retired and was given a send-off party by his colleagues. In that meeting many colleagues spoke about his several good qualities. But a Hindu peon in his speech said "we have seen in this officer's life the Jessu Swamy whom he worships" (In the official life of officers, more than any one, these peons and drivers will have opportunities to closely observe minute details). About this testimony which was like that of the angels who always watch all minute details of personal life of individuals, the officer said in his reply speech, "may it be for the glory of God and good of the people." About living like this according to the will of God, Jesus Christ himself says: "Jesus answered and said unto him, "If any man love me, he will keep my words: and my Father will love him and we will come unto him, and make our abode with him" (John 14:23).

Living in Universal Brotherhood is the Decisive Factor in the Final Judgement

St. John the Apostle shows the source of God's love which makes a child of God worthy of the glorious grace of abiding in God. This is a very prime factor that decides the fate of a human soul in the Life After Death: "Whosoever believeth that Jesus is the Christ, is born of God: and every one that loveth him that begat loveth him also that is begotten of him" (I John 5:1). This means, love all other men who are born of God, from the point of view that they are also the children of the Father in Heaven. The principle of universal brotherhood says that all mankind are any one's own brethren. The essence of the decisive factor in the Last Judgement would be revealed in the retrospection of how sincerely this commandment of love was practically observed in a human life. God's love beams abundantly in the lives of the truly faithful who have become God's children by abiding in him. How far this divine love has become practically operational in the actual life of a person decides his worthiness for entry into Heaven. In contradiction to this, "He that loveth not his brother abideth in death" (I John 3:14). "He that loveth not knoweth not God; for God is love" (I John 4:8). "If a man says, I love God, and hateth his brother, he is a liar for he that loveth not his brother whom he hath seen, how can he love God whom he hath not seen" (I John 4:20). Jesus Christ said : "Love your enemies, bless them that curse you" (Matt: 5:44).

The essence of the Ten Commandments which God has given in writing on the two stone tablets, is love to God and love to man. This will be the basis for the Last Judgement. During the life on this earth how much grace is earned by loving services rendered to fellow beings and carried to the Life After Death by a soul, is the primary decisive factor in the Final Judgement. "Blessed are the merciful for they shall obtain mercy" (Matt. 5:7). "For he shall have judgement without mercy, that hath showed no mercy and mercy rejoiceth against judgement" (James 2:13).

The divine eye will examine how God's love in us was manifested in our fraternal relationship with others. To respond to this with self-examination, St. John puts this question: "If a rich person sees his brother in need, yet closes his heart against his brother, how can he claim that he loves God?" (I John 3:17). The answer is in the next verse: "My children, our love should not be just words and talk; it must be true love which shows itself in action" (I John 3:18). Only the souls that have got intrinsic characteristic of life divine can identify itself with heaven which is the abode of love uttermost.

Preparedness to Face the Last Judgement with Hope

The divine words cited above are good exhortations to prepare ourselves in the earthly life itself to hopefully face the Last Judgement which is a very decisive event in the Life After Death. If we live a life radiant with divine love during the period given to us to live in the world, we will be able to hear the loving verdict of the judge sitting on the Judgement seat, welcoming us to the promised house of his Father. Otherwise his righteous judgement may come upon us as condemnation. God, just as he is an ocean of love, is also just righteous in his judgements.

9

Heaven, Hell, Paradise and Hades

THOUGH Heaven and Hell are separate subjects, to elucidate in comparison the differences between these two, both are dealt with under the same heading. Like that, Paradise and Hades also are dealt with in the same way.

No one living in this world has ever seen or reckoned these mysterious assignments or their whereabouts. Neither does anyone know for certain where they exist. We are accustomed to reckoning the location of anything or any place on earth or in the space in terms of the three dimensions of length, breadth and height. Similarly with regard to time, which is also infinite, we are used to reckoning the periodicity of occurrences by employing time calibrated measuring equipment like clock etc. in terms of hours, days, months, years, etc. as suitable for common man's mundane conception. But these are all limited to the mundane levels and suitable only to the poor understanding capacity of our sensual organs and faculties of our physical body in which we are in this physical world.

It is important to note that Heaven, Hell, Paradise and Hades are metaphysical entities and therefore they are not coming in the ambit of physical reckoning. To be more precise, they are spiritual entities belonging to the spiritual realm. Therefore they cannot be reckoned or understood by any physical parameters. Evidently these are spiritual experiences in the spiritual realm, in the respective situations thereof, in which a spirit of human soul, in simulating conditions, may reach. These are of spiritual dimensions which are quite different from physical dimensions. There are no words to define spiritual dimensions. Hence we should try to understand the spiritual meaning of the familiar words used to explain these spiritual mysteries in the real spiritual perspective. The Holy Spirit will guide us in this spiritual pursuit as we progress prayerfully in the study of the Holy Bible which gives definite hints to understand these mysterious entities.

Human beings getting a chance to live in this world in a material body with free mind and spirit which is the human soul, is a personality of triunity. This human being in his life in this world is on a probationary course with an aim in which the free will takes discretionary decisions for the performance of deeds which decide the development or damnation of the spiritual values with which it is created. How the spiritual stature of each individual personality is developed or damned, is the decisive factor by which the soul itself acquires the status to reach Paradise, Hades, Heaven or Hell. This can be understood from the revelations provided in the Holy Bible and explanations in these chapters 9, 10 and 11.

To Paradise or to Hades?

It is already stated that death, which is the door to pass from earthly life to eternity, does not open directly either to Heaven or Hell. "The wicked shall be turned into Hades and all the nations that forget God" (Psal. 9:17). "The way of life is above to the wise that he may depart from Hades beneath" (Prov. 15:24). A human soul, according to the degree of good or evil it has done in the tenure of life in this world, is constrained to go along with friends of identical nature. They may be God's messengers or Satan's messengers. But these two different types of messengers are not approaching only just to claim the soul when it leaves the body.

The Spiritual World that Encompasses Us

Along with every one there is a guardian angel right from the time of his birth, always within the reach of hand. Like that evil spirits also would be around. But we cannot see them with the eye of our earthly body. When our souls come out of our earthly body, with the spiritual eye we would be able to see the angels and the devils. Regarding infants, Jesus Christ has said: "That in Heaven their angels do always behold the face of my Father which is in Heaven" (Matt. 18:10). Every word or action of each individual is being observed very closely by the guardian angel and being promptly communicated to Heaven. Similarly, Satan and his hosts are also keenly observing the words and deeds of every human being and sending reports to their headquarters, about how a man has fallen into temptation.

Though these constant co-travellers will not be visible to our eyes, they are vying with each other to raise in us good or bad instigations by making use of or by creating suitable situations. While the hosts of Satan try to involve us in evil and sin, the angels of God, on bidding from God endeavour to build safety nets around us. "Then Satan answered the Lord, and said: Doth Job fear God for naught? Hast not thou made a Hedge about him, and about his house and about all that he hath on every side? . . ." (Job 1:9, 10).

In the Book of Life

In the earthly life, every talk and deed we do privately or publicly, are entered in the book of life kept by God. "And I saw the dead, small and great, stand before God; and the books were opened; and another book was opened, which is the book of life: and the dead were judged out of those things which were written in the books, according to their works" (Rev. 20:12). In these days of video discs and google scanning it is possible to record even minutest details of anything or any action from anywhere on the earth surface and see that on the personal computer. Similarly it is understandable that even in spiritual matters all details can be put on record in the spiritual realm. A devoted philosopher says: "*Each life automatically records itself your autobiography which is wrapped up within you and its pages are the epic of your life.*" For a soul which has done the deeds in the service of God or Satan, it is only possible to go with the servants of that master whom it has served during life. "No man can serve two masters . . ." (Matt. 6:24). *Remember, every idle word and even thought is recorded and we have to account thereof.* (Matt. 12:36 & 5:28) Psal 139:2.

There is None Righteous, no not One (Rom. 3:10)

It is impossible for anyone to live in this world in full spiritual perfection without doing anything wrong and be worthy of entering Heaven. But those who believed in Christ and acquired the grace of redemption by his atoning sacrifice cannot be claimed by the servants of Satan to be taken to the slavery of Hades. Because they are abiding in Christ and Christ abides in them, angels will usher them to Paradise without being seized by evil spirits that lurk in the space. Even in the course to Paradise the servants of Satan will bring false allegations against the souls which are justified ". . . Presumptuous are they, self-willed, they are not afraid to speak evil of dignities. Whereas angels which are greater in power and might, bring not railing accusation against them before the Lord" (II Peter 2: 10, 11). The spirits of true believers, who are saved by the grace of justification by their deeds and faith, enter Paradise. There they share the rich life of Christ and getting more and more sanctified become worthy of receiving the judgement of redemption to live in Heaven.

Hell-worthy Souls — Sin against the Holy Spirit

But those who deny God, indulging in sinful acts, utterly selfish, without any faith in God, will be claimed by the servants of that master whom they were obeying and serving in their lives on the earth. Like the soul of the rich man in the parable said by the Lord, they go to suffer the torments in the Hades. "For as many as have sinned without Law shall also perish without Law: and as many as have sinned in the Law shall be judged by the Law" (Rom. 2:12). *Even after knowing what is good and what is bad, those who deliberately sin against the Holy Spirit will not get repentance or remission of sins because of self-justification. The evil pleasure derived from sinful acts, would be cherished in the mind. This is worse than the act itself, by being instrumental in kindling unquenchable desires prompting further sinning. This condition prompts to fabricate reasons for self-justification, making repentance impossible. The Holy Spirit which guides human souls in all truth and righteousness cannot work its grace in such a condition where sinful desires are persistently cherished with self-justification by the will of the individual soul. In such a very serious situation it will not get remission of sins and grace of justification by faith and so will not get redemption at the Last Judgement.* "For if we sin willfully after that we have received the knowledge of the truth, there remaineth no more sacrifice for sins. But a certain fearful looking for judgement and of fiery indignation, which shall devour the adversaries" (Heb. 10: 26, 27). The passing then will be from Hades to Hell. There in Hell they become co-sufferers with Satan and his hosts in eternal condemnation. "Where their worm dieth not, and the fire is not quenched"

(Mark 9:48). Every one should try their utmost to avoid this condemnation. The tendency to endear in mind the evil pleasure to sin should be dislodged by deep-felt contrition, and confession, the most effective psychological remedy. ". . . make not provision for the flesh, to fulfill the lusts thereof" (Rom. 13:14).

The Righteousness of God that gives Opportunity to those who could not Know Christ in their Earthly Life, so that they may Know Him in the Life After Death

"For God judges everyone by the same standards." (Rom. 2:11)

Let us examine what the Holy Word says about the Salvation of those for whom it was not possible in this earthly life to know Jesus Christ fully or at least partly or believe in him or abide in him in the bond of love for him. If their life, by the prompting of their own conscience, is in accordance with the Law, there is no doubt that they will get recognition before God. (13) "For not the hearers of the Law are just before God, but the doers of the law shall be justified. (14) For when the Gentiles, which have not the Law do by nature the things contained in the Law, these, having not the Law, are a Law unto themselves. (15) Which shew the work of the Law written in their hearts, their conscience also bearing witness, and their thoughts, the meanwhile accusing or else excusing one another. (16) In the day when God shall judge the secrets of men by Jesus Christ according to my Gospel" (Rom. 2:13-16).

Grant of Special Grace in the Life After Death

As already mentioned in Chapter 5, the souls of those for whom it was not possible in their earthly life to know Christ or to believe and love him, will get an opportunity when they enter Sheol in Hades where the Omnipresent Saviour will be present. Even some very unrighteous people might have had some goodness. There they would be able to see him in spirit. Then those who believe, repent and take refuge in his saving grace will receive justification by faith added to their meager share of justification by deeds. Thus they will get the good fortune of getting adopted to life in Paradise by grant of the Saviour's grace of redemption on the merit of Christ's sacrifice. Adam and children got such graces for deliverance from Hades to Paradise (see Chapter 5). There they become partakers of the rich life of Christ and become worthy of the glorious status of abiding in him. Therefore we can believe that they would be receiving judgement of being justified and becoming heirs of the Kingdom of God. More details in this connection are given below:

Though Beloved Servants, for any Sins Due to Human Weakness there is Redemption on Merit of their Righteous Deeds

Though the earthly life was spent in devotion with love and service to God and fellow beings, who is there that has not fallen in any sin by the weakness of flesh or ignorance or the force of circumstances? It is certain that Satan will try to establish claim on such souls in the Life After Death. Moses the first among prophets and Joshua the Chief Priest, when they died, Satan tried to bring them under his custody. About this there are hints in the prophesy of Zechariah, Chapter 3 and Epistle of Jude Verse 9. While they were being accused for some silly sins the angel interfered and God rebuked Satan and they were freed and honoured. According to the message handed over by the angel they became worthy for the honour of the shining apparel of righteousness and life in Paradise.

Like that in the experience of St. Paul the apostle, he gets remission by grace for the mistakes he had committed by misunderstanding and lack of knowledge before believing in Christ "Who was before a blasphemer and a persecutor and injurious, but I obtained mercy, because I did it ignorantly in unbelief" (I Tim. 1:13). This, as he says, is the justification by faith in which the soul gets the grace thereof. Though this is an experience in his earthly life, it is seen that he believes that in the Life After Death also it will be accounted like that for the judgement of justification.

Justification by Faith is the Grace for Deliverance from Hades

The souls of all people, who died from the time of Adam till the death of Christ on the cross, were all sinful due to the original sin of the first father Adam by transgression of God's command, communicated to the generations behind, added with their own sinful deeds. All such souls which came under the captivity of Satan in Hades, heard the Good News of redemption by the sacrifice of Christ who shed his holy blood in propitiation of their sins. With repentance they believed and became worthy of the grace of justification by faith and got entry into Paradise (This is already explained in Chapter 5, quoting from I Peter 3: 8-19, 20-21). *The love and concern God shows towards his own creation, in not sending the souls of sinners immediately on their death to Hell but instead to the cleansing in Hades, to give them an opportunity for repentance and thereby granting them the grace of justification to be worthy of admission to Paradise, should not be disregarded*. "For he said to Moses, I will have mercy on any one I wish; I will take pity on anyone I wish" (Rom 9:15). In Life After Death, the grace of justification was granted only to those who believed in Christ. Love and faith that outlive death exist as the triumphant glory with the promise of the hope in redemption, till the day of the Last Judgement.

By Faith from Hades to Paradise

"God said to Moses, "I will have mercy on anyone I wish: I will take pity on anyone I wish." So then, everything depends, not on what man wants or does, but only on God's mercy" (Rom. 9:15, 16). The way to have the mercy of God is to believe in him and surrender to him in faith and contrition. That being entirely a spiritual exercise, even in the Life After Death, during the period of mercy, till the day of Last Judgement, it is at the merciful Will of God to redeem souls from Hades to Paradise. For grant of that grace those who are living in this world and the beloved departed in Paradise, offer intercessory prayers, as the most useful act of love. It is also an act that defeats Satan who is bent upon forcing death on human souls as the wages of sins committed as his servants in their earthly life.

Hades is the experience of spiritual darkness in which the hosts of Satan hold in captivity and torment the souls of such of the humans who in their earthly life were perpetrating evil deeds as His servants. Satan is a strict pay-master paying wages of sin in full measure which culminate in the soul's Spiritual death. Satanic hosts try all possibilities to detract the souls from the love and faith in God. But Christ declared that: "I am he that liveth and was dead; and, behold I am alive for evermore, Amen and have the keys of Hades and of death" (Rev. 1:18). Christ vanquished Satan and death for ever and his presence is victoriously established in Hades. In the radiation of his divine spiritual shining the human souls created in his image get enlightenment. This resuscitates their spiritual strength and those who listen to the Gospel of Salvation and believe in Christ will get released from the slavery of Satan and become worthy of getting the grace to live in Paradise. The authority which holds the keys of death and Hades has the right to enter there at any time. If not what meaning is there in possessing the key? Leaving the "ninety nine" who are the redeemed safe in Paradise the Good Shepherd, Christ, descends to Hades in search of the one that has wandered and lost the way. Finding it out in the perils of Hades, redeeming it from there, holding it close to his bosom, the Good Shepherd joins it with those which are in safety. None should attribute any limitation to this redeeming work of the Good Shepherd, the Saviour. However, only those who are willing to keep off the entanglements of sin and offer themselves into the saving hands of the Saviour would be getting the grace of Salvation. The sufferings endured in Hades would be counted as punishments for the sinful acts. This is what is taught through the parable of the rich man and Lazarus: (Luk. 16:19-25). Also see what the faithful David says in Psalm 49:15: "But God will redeem my soul from the power of the grave: for he shall receive me."* That is the redemption from Sheol (Hades).

Punishments Commensurate with the Seriousness of the Violation, is God's Righteousness in Redeeming Sinners from Hades

Relevant lessons from the parable of the master of the house and servants could be seen as follows:

The master of the house came while one servant was not mindful of the vigil he had to keep and behaved very bad and had to face the master at an unexpected moment. At that time, most unexpected, when men die and enter eternity to face God: "The servant who knows what his master wants him to do, but does not get himself ready and do it, will be punished with heavy whipping. But the servant, who does not know what his master wants and yet does something for which he deserves a whipping, will be punished with light whipping" (Luk. 12:47, 48).

---

* International Bible Commentary, p. 886.

As we could see from this parable, torments in Hades are adjusted as disciplinary measures to prepare the soul for eternity and could vary in severity depending on the measure of disobedience while on earth. Since the punishment is varying in intensity in each case as more or less, it is for improving by inducing self-examination, contrition, confession and change of heart. This is meant for improvement and not for condemnation to eternal doom in Hell. Such conditioning of the soul by temporary punishment before the Last Judgement added with the presence of the Saviour in Hades will kindle hope, faith and love in any sinner, clearing the way for accepting the grace for redemption to Paradise. So it is clear that the righteousness and mercy of God are manifest even in Hades to absolve sins and redeem human souls. Our intercessory prayers are most beneficial here for the departed souls.

Torments Leading to Contrition and Change of Heart

It is only fair to completely absolve a person from his guilt of a crime committed after he undergoes the punishment meted out for that. When the term of punishment is served the person becomes absolved and free of guilt. The justice which metes out the punishment recognizes the change of heart that comes in him. The soul of the rich man, who did not have mercy or any concern about the poor man who was suffering at his door, while suffering the torments in Hades, began to think about the Salvation of others. That shows the change of heart that has set in as a result of suffering the torments in Hades.

Christ the Good Shepherd who is having Steadfast Love is the Redeemer from Hades

In such circumstances as above, conducive to bring about repentance, the Holy Spirit of Christ the Good Shepherd comes in search of the sheep lost in the dangers of Hades. He has already declared: "I am the Good Shepherd. The Good Shepherd give his life for the sheep" (John 10: 11). The Good Shepherd, who gave his life on the cross to deliver human souls from the deadly hold of Satan, descended into Hades and redeemed them from Satan's bondage, to Paradise. It is verily what happens: "Now the God of peace that brought again from the dead, our Lord Jesus that great Shepherd of the sheep through the blood of the everlasting covenant" (Heb. 13: 20) has got this in His plan for redemption of human souls. *"For ye were as sheep going astray but are now returned unto the shepherd and Bishop of your souls"* (I Peter 2: 25). "And when the chief shepherd shall appear, ye shall receive a crown of glory that fadeth not away" (I Peter 5:4). This is the reward for obeying the call to the repentant sinner to Paradise where "unto everyone of us is given grace according to the measure of the gift of Christ" (Eph. 4:7). *"Wherefore he sayeth, when he ascended up on high, he led captivity captive and gave gift unto men"* (Eph. 4:8). *"Now that he ascended, what is it but he also descended first into the lower parts of the earth"* (Eph. 4: 9). *The Holy Word clearly reveals that Christ the Good Shepherd holding the key of Hades* (Ref: Rev. 1:18) *is ever watchful about the repenting sinners in torments of Hades to redeem them to Paradise till the day of Last Judgement*. This grace, as offered to Adam and his descendants, still remains extended to all human beings, irrespective of whether they belong to any caste, creed or religion, even to atheists who deny God. ". . . it was while we were still sinners that Christ died for us!" (Rom. 5: 8). "We were God's enemies, but he made us his friends through the death of his Son. . ." (Rom. 5: 10). God's love for his creation is uttermost in offering this last chance for all, of course, left to their free willed choice.

Sins for which Remission may be Granted or not Granted

However, Christ has said (please see chapter 6) that those who sin against the Holy Ghost will not get remission of sins there (Hades) also. The reason is that, because of arrogant self-justification they cannot get contrition and repentance and therefore no faith in God and His Salvation and become condemned for eternal damnation. There is no redemption from that situation. Apart from this, all other sins would be forgiven by repentance and faith. Therefore the departed souls who believe in Christ by their worship of God, supplications, contrition and intercessory prayers of others, sacrificial offerings etc., will acquire justification by faith and be redeemed from Hades to Paradise.

Diversities of Spiritual Virtues in the Glorious Life After Death

But those who are just saved from Hades because of faith and repentance brought about by the torment there and get a chance to enter Paradise will be poor in the glorious spiritual wealth expected of a child of God. They would be like those who were stripped off everything in a ship-wreck and just by sheer luck were washed ashore, grateful to be just alive. They would be in utter poverty with no adorable brilliance of excellence in spiritual character required for the glorious positions in eternal life of great happiness in Heaven, no adorning apparel of righteousness earned in a pure life of veritable deeds in the past, no inspiring stamp of personality that carries an air of kindness and faithfulness, no glitter of the brightness of truth and abundant spiritual life, no spiritual strength of steadfast faith and hope, no triumph of victories won over the world, flesh and Satan by absolute dependence on God's power, no spiritual fruitfulness of the adorable characteristics of peace, cheerfulness, mercy, charity, meekness, carefulness, sense of responsibility, truthfulness, punctuality, earnestness, self-control. With no enrichment of characteristics like long suffering, the grace of lowliness, firmness of faith, tranquility of peace or mental strength of forgiving grace. It is quite hopeful that in the period of merciful expectancy during the life in Paradise with true faith, supplications, contrition the intercessory prayers of others and by worshipping God, all such imperfections as above can be made up. The most important fact in this is the waking up of the faith in God resulting in contrition, true repentance to confess sins and offering supplication for pardon. By the plentifully granted grace of God, the worshipper gets the Wedding Garment. This is the specialty of this period of expectation in which the repentant believer gets from God the free gift of grace to participate in the "marriage feast of the Lamb of God" (Christ with the Church). If this opportunity also is not taken advantage of, it would not be possible to participate in the marriage feast of the Lamb of God.

Theophanic Inspirations Leading to Christophanic Revelations

> "No man can come to me, except the Father which hath sent me draw him" (John 6:44).

But those who are becoming worthy of approval for their righteousness in their earthly lives would get the grace of Theophanic Revelations due to justification by virtue of their faith and righteous deeds. Noah, Abraham, Moses, Elijah and such men were exceptional spiritual luminaries in their righteous life. They had intimate personal communion with God. Therefore Satan could not claim their souls into his slavery in Hades for torture after death. Unlike Adam and his sinful descendants, these righteous men had exceptional grace of justification by faith and deeds to enter Paradise even before Christ's sacrifice for redemption of human souls. To appear in celestial brightness on the mount of transfiguration with Jesus Christ, Moses and Elijah were not called from Hades, but they were coming from Paradise on a divine errand. Sure as anything, they were in Paradise in spiritual solace and glory by the grace of Theophanic communion with God the Father. In the parable of the rich man and Lazarus, as we can see from the description Christ has given (Luk. 16:23-26) that Abraham was not in Hades but in the lofty Paradise by virtue of Theophany.

All Righteous Souls, Irrespective of Caste, Creed or Nationality are Eligible for Paradise by the Grace of Christophany (See John 6:37)

This means, very righteous souls escape Hades and enter Paradise by virtue of Theophany leading to Christophany. Many persons from different places in the world acquire Theophanic virtue by righteous life; get celestial visions and guidance of the Holy Spirit of God, irrespective of any religion or nationality. They are guided to Christophanic grace according to God's own plan for each soul. One such example is the announcement of the angels to the shepherds about the birth of the "Saviour which is Christ the Lord" (Luk. 2:11). *Again, "came the wise men from the East of Jerusalem"* (Matt. 2:1) (India), *seeking the new born king of the Jews and wanting to worship him* (Mat 2:2). *By the Theophanic grace acquired by righteous life they are guided to the grace of Christophany, celebrated as epiphany, a church festival soon after Christmas.* All the righteous souls, irrespective of caste, creed or nationality, are eligible for entry into Paradise by grace of Christophany. Christians who happen to enter Paradise will probably be surprised to find there many many non-Christians who are guided by Christophanic grace as mentioned above. In this connection please see Chapter 5, pp. 77-81.

However, the malefactor who repented on the cross and acknowledged his faith in Christ directly received from him the grace of Christophany. This is one of the early instances of Christophanic revelation of redemption, due to justification by faith that merited his entry into Paradise to be with Christ. While it was with utter faith plus deep-rooted righteous life that people of Old testament days got Theophanic revelations of God enabling them to enter Paradise, in the days after Christ's sacrifice on the cross, the way to Paradise was wide open through Christ to all who believe in him and his propitiating sacrifice for all the world. That is the grace of Christophany on merit of justification by faith. But of course, to make amends for unrighteous deeds by human weakness there should be self-examination, contrition, confession, supplication and worship even while in Paradise. However, those who become worthy of the apparel of righteousness while in earthly life itself by their deeds, will become more radiant added by the grace of Christophany in Paradise, as Moses and Elijah. Let us try to enter the solace of Paradise with extra spiritual radiance by leading as much perfect righteous life as possible, while in this world.

Multi Faceted Individual Virtues in the Life After Death — Shining of the Righteous

"And they that be wise shall shine as the brightness of the firmament; and they that turn many to righteousness as the stars for ever and ever" (Dan. 12:3). According to the standards of quality maintained in the earthly life, the grace of glory that shines perpetually in the Life After Death will be in different degrees in different persons. It is like the difference in the glory between star to star (I Cor. 15:41).

In this connection it is worthy to recollect what is stated at the close of Chapter 6, that faith and practice should match (See James 2:22-24). Abraham's faith and deeds worked together. At the Last Judgement, the merit of righteousness in our deeds in the earthly life will be revealed. "For we must appear before the judgement seat of Christ; that every one may receive the things done in his body, according to that he hath done, whether it be good or bad" (II Cor. 5:10). Evidently, the apparel on the spiritual body acquired by every soul will be glorious or otherwise exactly according to each one's deed. Truly this glory is from the grace acquired by the soul and not due to reflection of any radiance of glory from outside. This is proved by what Jesus Christ has said: "Then shall the righteous shine forth as the sun in the Kingdom of their Father" (Mat 13:43). Others will not have any lustre of their apparel or perhaps no apparel even, as mentioned above.

Spiritual Virtues Acquired Immensely in Paradise, are Qualifying for Entry into Heaven

Paradise is a fellowship where the departed souls wait before the Last Judgement, expectantly hoping for entry into Heaven. Since there is the abiding presence of Christ, sanctification of the soul and renewal of spiritual life can be acquired by self-examination, contrition, confession, supplications and worship of God and intercessory prayers of other souls in the great family of God.

Necessary grace to enter Heaven should be acquired in the period of mercy while being in the Church expectant in Paradise. In the period of mercy this is possible for those souls in Hades also to come over to Paradise as a result of repentance induced by torments suffered there as punishment for unrighteous life as explained above. "For God judges every one by the same standard" (Rom. 2:11). The mind of the

Saviour who has identified himself with the father who was looking forward to receive the prodigal son who squandered everything he got as legacy from the father and coming back empty, shows how the loving redeemer is ready to receive repenting sinners. The lost virtues are quickly replenished in the redeemed soul and it is reinstated in the status of son in the family of God. When the lost son came back from the far country repenting for his evil ways he was received with love. He was clothed in the best robes with a ring on his hand and shoes for his feet and feast arranged in his honour. He was reinstated in parental love (Luk. 15:22). The Saviour has revealed through this parable how beautiful is the love of the Heavenly Father who loves the sinner but hates sin. Christ who has given his own blood in his sacrifice as propitiation for the sin of the world will not cast out even one soul which takes refuge in him. This is the great hope in the Glorious Life After Death. A loving Saviour awaits us in eternity which we enter by death.

The Magnificent Garment Merited by Acts of Righteousness — The Wedding Garment

The book of Revelations is one which presents a divine vision, depicting the human souls entering Life After Death, symbolically as bride and Christ as the bridegroom who, out of divine love, gave his Holy Blood as propitiating sacrifice to save her from spiritual death. The Church which is the bride has adorned herself with the clean shining robes granted to her by the grace of God. "And to her was granted that she should be arrayed in fine linen cleaned white: for the fine linen is the righteousness of saints" (Rev. 19:8). Like this, to be dressed in fine shining linen and to get the grace to participate in the wedding feast of the Lamb of God, let this thought inspire us to live in real righteousness. "You see, then that it is by his actions that a person is put right with God and not by his faith alone" (James 2:24). God is Love, but is righteous too. Therefore his judgement will be with love and righteousness.

But they who were Bidden were not Worthy (Matt. 22:8)

In a parable about the Kingdom of God, the master said to his servants: "the people invited for the wedding feast of his son's marriage had not come." So the servants were asked to go out into the streets and gather all people they could find. So, all the tribes are welcome to God's Kingdom. But only those who receive the invitation with preparedness of heart would be worthy to be admitted there. In order to participate in the wedding feast one should have the Wedding Garment. Very truly that is the adorning of the soul with the spiritual graces that are acquired through justification by faith and deeds in the physical life, grown richer while in Paradise. If such spiritual graces are not acquired while abiding in the Church Expectant in Paradise they will not be welcome in Heaven to participate in the wedding feast of the Lamb of God. Intense preparation is required for making amends for the spiritual poverty as explained above.

Without Wedding Garment

"The king went in to look at the guests and saw a man who was not wearing wedding clothes. "Friend, how did you get in here without wedding clothes? the king asked him. But the man said nothing. Then the king told the servants, tie him up hand and foot and throw him outside in the dark. There he will cry and gnash his teeth" (Matt. 22:11-13).

Attaining Perfection in Paradise the Place of Justification

On the scene of the happy wedding feast of the Lamb of God

in Heaven there is a very unhappy incident. One who gets in there without Wedding Garment is expelled. There is no admission in Heaven for those who try to enter there with unforgiven sin stains and no shining Wedding Garments. It may not be possible for anyone to be perfect as the Father in Heaven is perfect (Mat 5:48) to inherit Heaven as children of the Holy Father. But those who have sincerely and faithfully tried to attain that goal will be granted the grace of justification by faith during the period they wait as members of the expectant church in Paradise. Imperfections in sincere deeds in earthly life will be made up by the gracious Lord for granting grace of justification. The promise is assured in the Holy Word: "A bruised reed shall he not break and smoking flax he shall not quench" (Isaiah 42:3 & Matt. 12:20). Stains of sinful actions get cleansed by confession and surrender to the cross of Christ and the soul gets the Wedding Garment to be worthy of entering Heaven. Life in Paradise enhances the divine graces of the soul. Since the grace of redemption granted as the legacy of Sonship is abundantly showered on expectant souls in the utmost transparency and holiness of Paradise the souls are prepared there for the honour of living in Heaven as the children of the Lord God. If the period of expectation in Paradise for grant of justification by faith is not made use of for acquiring Wedding Garment, to be acquired by repentance and worship of God, the result will be merciless rejection from Heaven.

Those who are Ready to Receive the Bridegroom Went with Him to the Wedding Feast

As we can find from the parable of ten virgins who went out with their lamps to meet the bridegroom: "The five girls who were ready, went with him to the wedding feast and the door was closed" (Matt. 25:10). The other five whose lamps were going out for want of oil, could not accompany Christ the bridegroom to participate in the wedding feast in Heaven. They were rejected. The parable concludes with the warning "Watch therefore, for ye know neither the day nor the hour wherein the Son of man cometh" (Mat 25:13).

In the parable, the lamp stands for the faith and the oil for Grace of God acquired through a righteous life of loving deeds. Without oil lamp cannot be lighted. Like that faith alone is not enough to illuminate a soul. Belief is the first step towards faith. That is, one should believe in a fact to accept it as a matter of faith. A very specific example is here: Mark 5:2-13 narrates an incident in which the evil spirit in a man recognizes Jesus as the Son of God and screams for mercy not to torment it. St. James (2:19, 20) also states that the demons too believe this fact and tremble with fear. This shows that faith by itself is of no benefit except perhaps to instill fear of punishment. It is evident that the belief that Jesus is the Son of God is of no avail for the demon because he is an evil-doer full of hatred. Unless faith is shining forth through deeds of love and righteousness, it is dead like a lamp not lighted for want of oil. St. James states: "Even so faith, if it hath no works, is dead, being alone" (James 2:17). Again "You see then how that by works a man is justified and not by faith only" (James 2:24). Love is life. That is the motive force behind the graceful deeds of love and righteousness. These are deeds of individuals rendering services of love to others. The Grace of God acquired thus by one person cannot be shared with other to light his lamp of faith to get admitted to the marriage feast. As the period of deeds is over on entering the eternal life after death, it is wise to make life on earth worthwhile by utilizing opportunities for rendering loving service to our brethren, to be with God in Heaven in the Glorious Life After Death.

10

Heaven

NOBODY in this world has ever seen Heaven which is the centre of hope and goal of all religions. Though there are references in many places in the Holy Bible about this abode of God, any little description given by St. Paul is simply that ". . . eye hath not seen, nor ear heard, neither have entered into the heart of man, the things which God hath prepared for them that love him" (I Cor. 2:9). That perfect presence of His glorious face, we for lack of words call heaven, is beyond human conception or imagination. That spiritual ecstasy of personally experiencing the embrace of love divine is heaven which is beyond the understanding of anyone living in physical body in this world of physical limitations of space and time. Jesus Christ has said about this in his sermon on the mount "Blessed are the pure in heart: for they shall see God" (Matt. 5:8). From what our Lord has said very hopefully about the kingdom of God, to his disciples before his crucifixion, we can understand something about the experience of the ultimate spiritual solace promised for human souls in that state of Glorious Life After Death. Of course, this experience should begin in this life itself to be continued in its perfection in the life eternal.

An Absolutely Trustworthy Promise

Moments before going to the garden of Gethsemane where the soldiers of Jewish priests arrested Jesus, he told his disciples these words of promise to be remembered by all the faithful: "Let not your heart be troubled: Ye believe in God, believe also in me. In my Father's house are many mansions: if it were not so, I would have told you. I go to prepare a place for you. And if I go and prepare a place for you, I will come again and receive you unto myself: that where I am, there ye may be also" (John 14:1-3). In Heaven are the mansions which are being prepared by Lord Jesus Christ in the house of his Father in Heaven for the human souls to live. Therefore it is enough to know this much about Heaven. If one reaches there, the happiness therein to be understood and enjoyed is something beyond the comprehension of anyone. At this, disciple Thomas asks an innocent question: "Lord, we do not know where you are going; so how can we know the way to get there?" (John 14:5). *Jesus answered him, "I am the way the truth and the life; no one goes to the Father except by me"* (John 14:6).

Christ the Only Way to Reach Heaven

A way is a passage that links one place with another for travel to and fro. The way to Heaven is also like that. When Christ says that he himself is the way for us to go to Heaven, and to get the grace of acceptance coming that way, he means exactly that itself. *When Christ's humaneness in this world stands at the lowly level of man, his Godliness holds out at the Heavenly grandeur of glory. In his incarnation as human, he was God with us (Emmanuel). The Son of the most high and exalted God himself descended to the lowliest level of being the Son of Man by his incarnation in human body for gifting the grace of redemption to human race. And he was revealing the divine secret of Salvation he is going to offer man by lifting man with himself to the lofty heights of the Sonship of God, by presenting before the Father his blood-fresh wounds and pleading for our redemption (Ref. Rom. 8:34), identifying himself as the way to God the Father. As the scripture says, "When He went up to the very heights, he took many captives with him. . ."*

(Eph. 4:8). The Son of God who became the Son of man in his incarnation, and gave himself to us as the bread of life to abide in us and we in him, makes the way for us to Heaven where he is on the right hand of God the Father. Through him we are received as sons of God.

The Excellence Required for Entry into Heaven

"Not everyone that sayeth unto me, "Lord, Lord, shall enter into the Kingdom of Heaven; but he that doeth the will of my Father which is in Heaven. Many will say to me in that day, Lord, Lord, have we not prophesised in thy name? and in thy name have we not cast out devils? and in thy name done many wonderful works? And then will I profess unto them, I never know you: depart from me, ye that work iniquity. . ." (Matt. 7:21-23). But how we frail human beings can know the will of God? Of course, we have the promise of getting guidance of Holy Spirit of God to know the will of God and live accordingly (See the promise in Luk. 11:13, John 14:26 & Rom. 5:5). On the Last Judgement day each one gets the judgement he deserves. See how Jesus Christ has stated about the love of God that awaits to welcome the heirs to Heaven, in his own words: "Then the King will say to the people on his right "Come you that are blessed by my Father; come and possess the Kingdom which has been prepared for you ever since the creation of the world" (Matt. 25:34).

Deserving the Father's Blessings

Heaven is the place of spiritual happiness that God prepared for those who love him. It is only by the blessing of God that we would be able to inherit it. Our worthiness for the blessing of God is dependent upon the selfless services of love that we render to our brethren during our life in this world. This is very clearly brought out by our Lord Jesus Christ in the simple dialogue cited in the following paragraph.

"Inasmuch as ye have Done it unto One of the Least of these my Brethren ye have Done it unto me" (Matt. 25:40)

"Then the king will say to the people on his right, come, you that are the blessed by my Father: Come and possess the Kingdom which has been prepared for you ever since the creation of the world. I was hungry and you fed me, thirsty and you gave me a drink; I was stranger and you received me in your homes, naked and you clothed me; I was sick and you took care of me, in prison and you visited me." The righteous will then answer him, "when, Lord did we ever see you hungry and feed you or thirsty and give you a drink? When did we ever see you a stranger and welcome you in our homes or naked and clothe you? When did we ever see you sick or in prison and visit you?" *The King will reply, "I tell you, whenever you did this for one of the least important of these brothers of mine, you did it for me!"* (Matt. 25:34-40).

Oh! What a great grand opportunity for us in this transient human life on this earth to work for and acquire the glorious eternal legacy of God's Sonship in his Kingdom through simple acts of love towards our brethren! *Let us be constantly watching for opportunities to render such loving services of mercy and kindness to anyone, even to our enemies, as we are passing through this way only once in this life.*

Perfect Justification by Faith and Action

As stated at the beginning of this book in chapter 1, "God who is love uttermost, sharing from his infinite spirit of love, created man conferring on him perfect individuality with a mind of free will, for loving him and for him to love." Therefore the real worthiness to live with Him in Heaven is for those who have proved their love in actual physical life on the earth. The grace of Sonship that is bestowed through justification by faith and supported by justification by deeds in a life of mercy and love makes us worthy of the blessing thereof in eternal Life After Death. God gives this as his free gift of blessing to believers who are also righteous. Father gives blessings to children. That blessing is the free inheritance to the Sonship in the Kingdom of God. While writing these lines this unworthy servant is self-examining his own life with deep feelings and determination to make his own life still more mellowed with charity, invoking the divine notes of love in I Cor.Ch. 13. The grace of justification by faith is a free gift. Adding along with it the grace of justification by deeds will give the human souls divine lustre and glory in the Life After Death. God has eternity in the heart of men and so we set our minds forward looking into the vast unknown.

Action-oriented Life on Earth is the Training Period to Attain Covetable Positions in Heaven

God gives a sufficient lifetime to everyone to earn spiritual grace of justification by faith supported by deeds of love. We have to be very dedicated and earnest in utilizing our talents as opportunities present themselves to be used for the glory of God and good of the world. *Sloth is one of the seven deadly sins. There is no place for idlers in the Kingdom of God. There is no second chance for anyone, as some people wrongly say that a person who lived in a previous generation has taken re-birth in a subsequent generation. Why only some persons are given such a chance? Is God partial? Satan who can see through all past generations can give vivid "convincing" details in the minds of some people as if they remember details of previous life. People are misled as in the case of King Saul* (Ch. 2:19 and 20). *They are enticed to careless living without serious thought of the once-for-all a lifetime chance to be made worthy of reaching Heaven's solace* (See Chapter 1). Any chance of correction by grace of justification is in Hades or

Paradise — vide Chapter 6. *The factual drama of life in this world is not a rehearsal for corrective repetitions.*

Parable of the Talents — Positions of Honour in the Life After Death

Jesus Christ has taught through a parable that the proper use of the different talents given to people in the earthly life will be the yardstick for grant of high honours in the Glorious Life After Death in the Kingdom of God (Matt. 25:14-30). Here is the parable: A rich man before he set out for a far country, called his servants and entrusted to them portion of his wealth. To one he gave five talents, to another two talents and to another one talent, according to the ability of each. The one who got five talents immediately went off, invested it in some business and earned another five talents. The one who got two talents also earned another two talents. But the one, who got only one talent, made a pit in the ground and buried the talent therein. After some time when the master returned and asked the accounts, the one who got five talents said he has earned another five. Then his master congratulated him and said "Well done, you good and faithful servant, you have been faithful in managing a few things, so I will make you ruler over many things, enter the joy of the master. Like that the second who got two talents said he earned another two talents. He was also congratulated like that. But the one who got one talent said he buried it. The master was angry and ordered to take back the one talent from him and cast him to the darkness outside.

Development of One's Born Talents and their Dedication

People who are born with different abilities should develop them to their best during their life on earth and thus lead a life that would be for the glory of God and good of the world. Beyond that, it is to be understood that in the Glorious Life After Death also it would be a factor to decide our worthiness for varied responsible positions in the Kingdom of God. In Heaven, according to divine vocation, positions of great responsibilities are waiting for us. If we could dedicate ourselves entirely to the creator in carrying out such services of love while on earth, that will be worthwhile. It is the self-dedication which Heaven welcomes. *"What you are is God's gift to you and what you are to be is your gift to God."* Therefore let us strive to develop our God-given talents in this life to excel in the high placements in the Kingdom of God in the high status as sons of God (See Chapter 12).

Child-like Dependence Makes Dedication Blessed

Having offered all the abilities that are developed in the earthly life as offering to God, there is nothing else as one's own. We have only to depend upon God entirely. Here is the secret of being blessed. It is like the guiltless infant who completely relies upon parents. This is what Jesus Christ has revealed to his disciples as the prime quality required for entering Heaven. *"I assure you that unless you change and become like children, you will never enter the Kingdom of Heaven"* (Matt. 18:3). This change of heart will show itself in life, in characteristics of gentleness and cheerfulness as the best part of one's religion. With such a change in heart, our souls acquire the grace of getting the loving welcome to be in the perfect presence of God's Glorious face which is Heaven. From this it has to be understood that the coming back to the child-like innocence and pristine purity of heart and a life completely dedicated to God and entirely depending upon Him, will be sanctified and blessed by God to make us worthy to enter Heaven.

11

Hell

HELL is abhorred by all people as the experience of punishment in eternal doom reserved for Satan and his hosts. Let us close this book with exhortations for not falling into the experience of Hell to be doomed to the eternal torments and damnation in that state of the soul. Sufficient warning is given under Chapter 5 captioned as "Danger Signals in the Life After Death." In the Bible there are very many warnings against falling into miserable experience of Hell in which the unfortunate souls who, having failed to receive any justification by faith and good deeds, receive the judgement of condemnation on the day of Last Judgement.

Hell the Experience of Sans Love in which Lust and Selfishness Predominate

In the absence of even an iota of love, God who is love is not sought after in the experience sans love in Hell. It is the headquarters of Satan. Those who in their earthly life were loveless and utterly selfish are destined to go to a life suitable for their nature of lust and selfishness. *Regarding the undying worm and unquenchable fire, note the words of our Lord: "Where their worm dieth not and the fire is not quenched"* (Mark 9:44). *It means that undying worm is of the sufferers' own making for them. The Hell-fire is also not kindled by any fuel provided from elsewhere. That fire is also of the Hell-worthy souls' own intrinsic development of their sinful passions like lust, hatred, revenge, jealousy, etc. burning in them and consuming them incessantly. Their ever-grabbing worm of undying and insatiate sinful desires and greed lurking in them torment them forever, making Hell for their souls.* Thus Hell is the most unfortunate state created by oneself. This begins from a loveless, selfish and sinful earthly life with no compunction and repentance in which spiritual life of the soul ebbs out to extinction beyond any possibility of recovery or redemption, which is the eternal punishment. No more chance to repent after the Last Judgement in which the cursed life is condemned. To them God says "Away from me, you are under God's curse; away to the eternal fire which has been prepared for the Devil and his angels! I was hungry but you would not feed me, thirsty but you would not give me a drink; I was a stranger but you would not welcome me in your home, naked but you would not clothe me; I was sick and in prison but you would not care for me. Then they will answer him, "When Lord did we ever see you hungry or thirsty or stranger or naked or sick or in prison and we would not help you." *The King will reply "I tell you, whenever you refused to help one of these least important ones, you refused to help me."* Those then, will be sent off to eternal punishment, but the righteous will go to eternal life (Matt. 25:41-46).

He who does not Show Mercy will not Get Mercy

In the parable of the rich man and Lazarus the Lord says, "There was a certain rich man, which was clothed in purple and fine linen and fared sumptuously every day" (Luk. 16:19). There is no hint that he committed any other sin. But he had no concern about the suffering of Lazarus a sick beggar lying at his door step. He was so sick and poor that dogs were licking the wounds of his naked body. Even though the rich man had enough resources to render the necessary human services to that poor sufferer he did not care for that. Instead he lived happily in utter selfishness with his riches every day. Lazarus was left to die without getting any care. Only that negligence of not caring for the poor man perishing in his sight was enough to send the rich man to the torments of Hades. It is our duty to look out for the destitute brethren suffering around us and render them necessary help in loving service. We should never be negligent about it. Without wasting any such opportunity we should carry out such human services of love diligently. Depending upon our response to such duty calls we would be ourselves beginning either Heaven or Hell in ourselves for the Life After Death.

The way to Hell is Pleasant and Easy

No one needs to take trouble searching to know where Hell is. Those who welcome and usher people to that life are the numerous hosts of Satan. Identifying other people and opportunities and tactfully tempting with enticing words, they would charm the victim towards the path to Hell of unquenchable sinful passions.

"Suddenly he was going with her like an ox on the way to be slaughtered, like a deer prancing into a trap, where an arrow would pierce its heart. He was like a bird going into a net — he did not know that his life was in danger (Prov. 7:22, 23).

Damnation of Hell

Jesus Christ asked a vital question to the scribes and Pharisees addressing them as "Ye serpants, ye generation of vipers, how can ye escape the damnation of Hell?" (Matt.23:33). Instead of taking this as a warning and call for repentance they were plotting to kill Jesus. Jesus rebukes them openly calling them hypocrites and detailing their wrong doings as seen in the earlier verses of this chapter (Matt. 23; 34-36). Here Jesus gives a hint about Hell and its damnation waiting for evil doers.

Hell is a self-doomed state created by man in himself by his evil deeds. This is the result of self-justification, in utter selfishness and absence of love, by which the conscience becomes hardened in sinful conditions without any repentance or compunction. So the soul continues in sinful conditions. This is sin against the Holy Spirit, which has no remission. An evil soul bears its own Hell with it. It is not God's fault. A Hell-making soul, not changing its attitude, if summoned to Heaven will not stay there. It prefers to go Satan's way. It is truly said of *Satan's lamentation*: *"Wherever I turn is Hell, Myself am Hell." It is the soul's own mind setup, as described above, by which it chooses its own way to Hell*. How the soul falls into such an unfortunate fate is explained in Chapter 5, pp. 84-85.

12

Conclusion

Eternal Vigilance Against Satan's Hatred

As stated in the beginning of this book, God who is absolute love, gifting from his infinite spirit of love, created man as a perfect individual person with a mind of free will to love him and for him to love. He cannot bear any one human soul being lost. ". . . *God so loved the world that he gave his only begotten Son, that whosoever believeth him should not perish, but shall have everlasting life*" (John 3:16). That is why the Son of God became incarnate as Man and shed his Holy Blood in propitiating sacrifice, died, resurrected and opened the way to Salvation for sinners. But remember, the most eminent angel of light, Lucifer who fell from that position and became Satan, is in perpetual jealousy and revenge towards man who is created to occupy his lost position. He is always trying to entice man by any means to sin and become co-sufferer with him in Hell. His modus operandi is to arouse rebellious attitude in men and induce them to act against God's love and design, to be condemned and thrown into Hell. To prevent sinners from repentance and remission of sins, Satan would be inciting them to harden their minds in self-justification and unbelief in God. Continuing like that with un-remitted sins the souls receive death as the wages of sin. "*The wage of sin is death; but the gift of God is eternal life through Jesus Christ our Lord*" (Rom. 6:23). Therefore "Be sober, be vigilant: because your adversary the devil, as a roaring lion, walketh about seeking whom he may devour" (I Peter 5:8). So, take the warning to lead a Heaven-worthy life while in this world and avoid the torments in Hades or Hell.

The Righteous shall Shine Like the Sun

But Christ has said that those who lead righteous lives without falling into satanic temptations are God's people. They acquire the grace of justification through good deeds and faith in Him. "Then shall the righteous shine like the sun in their Father's Kingdom" (Matt. 13:43). Do not be surprised when some simple people who lived inconspicuous common life in this world are seen very glorious in the Life After Death. That is the magnificence which the Lord promised and what they receive. When the reason for this is understood the surprise will change to gladness.

To Higher and more Glorious Status than Archangels as Sons of God

"What are the angels, then? They are spirits who serve God and are sent by Him to help those who are to receive Salvation" (Heb. 1:14). *But God abides in humans whom he has redeemed to Heavenly life by giving them his Holy Blood: "But as many as received him, to them gave he power to become the Sons of God, even to them that believe in his name: Which were born, not of blood, nor of the will of the flesh nor of the will of man but of God"* (John 1:12-13). *These verses bear spiritual meaning.* This great blessing is received by human souls not by any physical observances but by divine love and faith in the guidance of the Holy Spirit leading to the glorious hope. "For as many as are led by the Spirit of God, are the Sons of God" (Rom 8:14).

Heirs of God and Joint Heirs with Christ

It cannot be overlooked that in the Glorious Life After Death, human souls, as children of God, have a much higher and more glorious position than angels and archangels who are ministering spirits sent forth to minister for them who shall be heirs of Salvation. Sons of God have special blessings befitting the high positions they have to adorn in the Kingdom of God as his heirs in Sonship. In his first epistle to Corinthians, St. Paul asks: *"Know you not that we shall judge angels?"* (I Cor. 6:3). The reason is that the Holy Spirit of God, who guides in all truth and righteousness, abides in us in Sonship. This is a fact which we should always hold in our minds with awe. *"And if children, then heirs, heirs of God and joint heirs with Christ"* (Rom. 8:17). In the prayer which our Lord has taught us beginning with the salutation: "Our Father which art in Heaven" (Matt. 6: 9), confirms our Sonship. Jesus Christ taught us to pray "Thy kingdom come" so that the heirs of the kingdom may work and pray for the progress of the Heavenly Father's Kingdom. First that Kingdom should start with its domain in our hearts in this earthly life itself and spread in infinite dimensions to eternity.

Glory of the Redeemed Souls in the Life After Death

Since the honour of being the Sons of God has been given to the redeemed souls but not even to the archangels, in the Glorious Life After Death we will be in positions higher than the archangels. Never forget that we are going to see God our Heavenly Father face to face (I Cor. 13: 12) while we enter our inheritance as Sons of God in Heaven. To prepare new mansions befitting such higher glories in his Father's house, Jesus Christ resurrected and ascended to Heaven. But only after the Last Judgement there is admission there. What is the state of such happiness? That is beyond anybody's imagination. To inherit such great glory we have to lead a beautiful love-filled life while here. So for that, let us sincerely try to make best use of the time we get in this life by leading a life of love and righteousness for the good of the world and Glory of God in whom we have hope of a Glorious life in eternity.

Love Welcomes Love

What can we give in return to this great love of God which redeems us from the curse of sin and death to such a precious legacy of his Sonship in life eternal? Our Faith, Gratitude, Devotion, Obedience, Offerings, Sacrifices, Praise? These are all inadequate. God desires our love — pure love only. For that only man was created to share the spirit of God's divine love. The first and greatest of God's commandments is also this. "Love the Lord your God with all your heart, with all your soul and all your mind (Matt. 22:37, Mark 12:30, 33, Luk. 10:27). Christ confirms about love that should exist among men: ". . . to love his neighbour as himself is more than all whole burnt offerings and sacrifices" (Mark 12:33). The meaning of this shines out in the context of what is stated by Christ himself that: ". . . Verily I say unto you, inasmuch as ye have done it unto one of the least of these my brethren ye have done it unto me" (Matt. 25:40). This is so beautifully corroborated in the epistle of St. Paul to Romans "Love worketh no ill to his neighbour: therefore love is the fulfilling of the Law" (Rom. 13:10). Faith, devotion, obedience, worship and offerings all attain perfection by love. Jesus Christ said: "therefore if thou bring thy gift to the altar and there rememberest that thy brother has ought against thee: Leave there thy gift before the altar and go thy way; first be reconciled to thy brother and then come and offer thy gift" (Matt. 5:23, 24). During the life in this world the love towards our brethren exhibited through deeds of loving services will grow to the glory of God accepting us. Anything to be acceptable in Heaven should be prompted by love. Return of the prodigal son, even from the midst of all troubles and losses, was prompted by love. The Father's love goes out promptly in welcome and receives the returning prodigal son. What is pleasing to the love of God which redeemed humanity from the doom of sin and death is the pure love of the human soul towards God. That cannot be shared with anything else. Then the human life becomes worthwhile in the house of the Father in Heaven.

Death is the Door that Opens the Way Through Christ to the Eternal Bliss

Let us be prepared always for the blessed happiness of this glorious meeting at any time. Individual death or the second coming of the Lord may be at any unexpected moment. Therefore, attaining justification by deeds of love and faith, let us be hopefully ready for meeting the Lord. Let us not forget what Jesus Christ himself said about this: "For the Son of Man is as a man taking a far journey, who left his house and gave authority to his servants and to every man his work and commanded the porter to watch. Watch therefore; for ye know not when the master of the house cometh, at even or at midnight or at the cockcrowing or in the morning. Lest coming suddenly he find you sleeping" (Mark 13:34-36).

"Let your loins be girded about and your lights burning" (Luk. 12:35). "Blessed are those servants, whom the Lord when he cometh shall find watching; verily I say unto you, that he shall gird himself and make them sit down to meat and will come forth and serve them" (Luk. 12:37). *"Be ye therefore ready also; for the Son of Man cometh at an hour when you think not"* (Luk. 12:40). "And what I say unto you I say unto all, WATCH" (Mark 13:37).

I pray that the Holy Spirit of God may give inspiration and guidance to all human beings through this little book to get prepared and be watching for the moment of our Lord calling us to the extremely Glorious Life with Him in Heaven that awaits us in the Life After Death.

Bless us Oh Lord Jesus Christ
Crucified for us.

Mṛtyor ma amṛtaṁ gamaya
From death lead me to Immortality

Table of Bible Quotations

Page No.	SI. No.	Book Ref.	Chapter & Verse	Bible Version
1	1	Gen.	2:7	KJV
	2	Psal.	8:5	" "
	3	Psal.	139:14	" "
2	4	Gen.	1:24	GNB
	5	" "	1:27	" "
	6	" "	2:7	" "
3	7	" "	1:24	" "
4	8	II Pet.	2:4	KJV
	9	Jude	V:6	" "
	10	Psal.	8:5	GNB
	11	" "	139:14	KJV
5	12	I Cor.	3:16, 17	KJV
8	13	Psal.	90:10	GNB
	14	Gen.	5:5-27	" "
	15	" "	6:3	" "
10	16	II Timo.	4:7, 8	KJV
	17	Gen.	2:17	KJV
	&		& 3:6	& GNB
	18	Gen.	3:22	" "
12	19	Mark	14:21	KJV
	20	Luk.	22:22	" "
	21	Matt.	27:4	" "
15	22	Phillipi,	1:29	KJV
	23	Rom.	8:35	" "
	24	I cor.	10:13	" "
	25	I Pet.	4:1	" "
	26	I Pet.	1:6, 7	" "
	27	James	1:12	" "
15	28	Psal.	119:71	KJV
	29	Isiah	38:17	" "
16	30	Mark	5:41	" "
	31	Luk.	7:14, 15	" "
	32	John	11:39	" "
24	33	Luk.	16:22	KJV
	34	John	8:12	" "
25	35	Luk.	24:12	" "
	36	John	20:5-7	" "
	37	Matt.	17:2	" "
	38	Mark	9:3	" "
	39	Luk.	9:29	" "
26	40	Gen.	3:21	GNB
	41	Deut.	8:4 & 29:5	" "
	42	Luk.	16:23-28	" "
27	43	" "	23:43	KJV
	44	Colos.	3:3	KJV
	45	Luk.	16:23	" "
	46	" "	16:24-26	" "
29	47	Psal.	15:1-3	" "
	48	Psal.	24:3, 4	KJV
	49	Matt.	5:48	" "
30	50	John	10:11	GNB
	51	" "	10:3	" "
34	52	IPet.	5:8	KJV
35	53	Exod.	22:18	GNB
	54	I Sam.	28:8	" "

Page No.	Sl. No.	Book Ref.	Chapter & Verse	Bible Version
35	55	I Sam.	28:16, 19	GNB
	56	" "	31:3-5	" "
	57	Gen.	3:4, 5	GNB
37	58	II Cor.	11:14	" "
40	59	I Sam.	3:10	KJV
42	60	Luk.	16:22, 23	GNB
45	61	I Cor.	2:9	KJV
52	62	Psal.	36:9	" "
54	63	John	8:12	" "
59	64	Matt.	17:4	" "
	65	Mark	9:5	" "
	66	Luk.	9:33	" "
	67	Matt.	21:28	" "
61	68	I Cor.	13:12	GNB
62	69	Luk.	8:54	" "
	70	Luk.	7:22	" "
	71	John.	11:11-13	" "
67	72	Psal.	42:1, 2	KJV
	73	" "	50:7	" "
	74	" "	63:1	" "
	75	John	14:2, 3	" "
68	76	" "	11:26	" "
	77	" "	16:5	GNB
	78	John	16:7, 8	KJV
	79	Psal.	15	" "
	80	I Cor.	2:9	" "
69	81	John	11:11	" "
	82	Luk.	8:52	" "
	83	II Cor.	5:10	" "
	84	Matt.	5:29, 30	KJV
70	85	Mark.	9:43-49	" "
71	86	I Cor.	15:49	KJV
	87	Luk.	23:43	" "
	88	Rom.	6:2	" "
	89	" "	6:3	GNB
72	90	" "	6:4	" "
72	91	Colos.	3:3	KJV
73	92	I Pet.	3:18, 19	GNB
	93	" "	" "	" "
74	94	" "	3:20, 21	" "
	95	I Pet.	3:19	GNB
	96	" "	3:22	" "
75	97	I Pet.	4:5	GNB
	98	Heb.	9:22	KJV
76	99	Matt.	20:1-16	GNB
	100	Matt.	20:15	" "
	101	" "	5:48	" "
	102	Isiah	64:6	KJV
	103	Ephes.	2:8, 9	GNB
77	104	Rom.	8:34	" "
	105	Heb.	7:25	" "
	106	I Cor.	12:3	KJV
78	107	John	10:16	GNB
	108	Rev.	1:18	KJV
	109	Isaiah	49:6	" "
	110	I John	2:2	" "
	111	Matt.	8:8	" "
	112	" "	8:10-12	" "
79	113	" "	7:21, 23	" "
	114	Matt.	21:31	KJV
	115	" "	21:32	" "
80	116	I Pet.	3:20, 21	GNB
	117	I Cor.	10:1, 2	" "
	118	Acts	11:16-18	GNB
81	119	I Pet.	3:20	" "
	120	Matt.	5:48	" "
	121	Matt.	12:21	" "
	122	Isiah	42:3	KJV
	123	Matt.	12:20	" "
82	124	John	3:8	GNB
	125	Rom.	10:9, 10	GNB
83	126	Heb.	11:6	" "
	127	Heb.	11:1	KJV
84	128	Luk.	23:39	" "

Page No.	Sl. No.	Book Ref.	Chapter & Verse	Bible Version
85	129	Matt.	12:31	" "
	130	Mark	3:28, 29	" "
	131	Luk.	12:10	" "
87	132	Psal.	40:7	" "
	133	Heb.	10:7	" "
	134	Luk.	4:14-21	GNB
88	135	Matt.	2:1, 9-11	KJV
	136	Rom.	10:9	" "
	137	Heb,	1:1	KJV
89	138	Deut	15:9	" "
91	139	Colos.	3:3	KJV
	140	Psal.	115:18	KJV
	141	John	15:5	" "
	142	Psal.	115:17	" "
92	143	" "	115:17	" "
	144	" "	115:18	" "
	145	Rev.	7:15	" "
	146	John	4:24	" "
	147	John	15:4	KJV
93	148	" "	14:6	" "
	149	" "	4:21	" "
	150	" "	4:23	" "
94	151	Psal.	27:4	KJV
	152	" "	27:8	" "
95	153	Isiah	6:1-8	KJV
96	154	Heb	10:39	" "
	155	John	15:5	" "
	156	Matt.	5:48	KJV
97	157	John	3.16	" "
	158	Rom.	8:34	" "
	159	Heb.	7:25	" "
	160	Heb.	12:24	" "
98	161	Luk.	16:27, 28	KJV
	162	Acts	7:55, 56	GNB
	163	Heb.	12:1	" "
	164	" "	12:21	" "
99	165	" "	12:22-24	" "
99	166	Acts	6:15	KJV
	167	John	17:23	KJV
100	168	" "	17:20	" "
	169	James	5:16	" "
	170	Rev.	7:15	" "
101	171	John	2:1-11	" "
	172	John	2:3	KJV
102	173	" "	2:4	" "
	174	John	2:11	KJV
	175	" "	2:9	" "
	176	Prov.	15:29	" "
103	177	Rom.	8:15	" "
	178	Rom.	8:26	KJV
	179	Rom.	8:27	" "
	180	Rom.	8:28	KJV
105	181	Matt.	5:48	" "
	182	Isaiah	64:6	" "
	183	James	2:24	GNB
106	184	James	2:21-23	KJV
	185	II Cor.	5:10	" "
	186	Matt.	5:48	" "
	187	Rom.	3:10-12	" "
	188	Rom.	3:23	" "
107	189	Numbers	21:5,6	KJV
	190	" "	21:9	" "
108	191	I Pet.	2:24	GNB
	192	Rom.	10:11	" "
	193	Rom.	10:9	" "
	194	Luk.	1:54, 69,70	GNB
109	195	Rom.	7:8	GNB
	196	Rom.	7:9	" "
	197	" "	7:10	" "
	198	" "	7:19-21	" "
	199	" "	3:24	KJV
	200	" "	3:27, 28	" "
110	201	Heb.	9.22	KJV
	202	" "	9:9, 10	GNB
	203	" "	9:26	KJV

Page No.	SI. No.	Book Ref.	Chapter & Verse	Bible Version
111	204	Matt.	26:26, 27	GNB
	205	Mark	14:22-24	" "
	206	Luk.	22:19, 20	" "
	207	Luk.	22:19	KJV
112	208	" "	23:42	" "
	209	" "	23:43	" "
	210	Gen.	9:8-17	" "
113	211	Coloss.	2:9	KJV
	212	Lev.	2:1	KJV
	213	" "	4:25	" "
	214	" "	5:6	" "
	215	" "	7:15	" "
	216	" "	7:30	" "
	217	" "	2:10	" "
	218	" "	5:13	" "
	219	" "	6:16, 26	" "
	220	" "	8:31	" "
114	221	John	6:48	" "
	222	John	6:51	KJV
	223	" "	6:53, 54	" "
	224	" "	6:56	" "
	225	" "	6:57, 58	" "
115	226	I Pet.	2:24	GNB
	227	Psal.	32: 1, 2	GNB
	228	Rom.	4:5-8	" "
116	229	I Cor.	13:12	" "
117	230	I Thess.	5:17	KJV
118	231	Ephe.	4:32	" "
	232	Gal.	6:1	KJV
	233	I Pet.	3:18	GNB
	234	Rom	5:8	" "
	235	" "	5:10	" "
	236	John	13:34	KJV
119	237	Rom.	5:5	GNB
120	238	Exodus	28:9, 10	KJV
	239	" "	28:29	" "
	240	Ruth	2:20	" "
	241	II Maccab.	12:41, 42	" "
121	242	" "	12:43	KJV
	243	" "	12:44	" "
	244	" "	12:45	" "
	245	II Timo.	1:16	GNB
	246	" "	1:18	" "
122	247	II Cor.	5:10	GNB
123	248	Matt.	12:31, 32	KJV
124	249	Song of Songs	1:4	KJV
	250	SS.	2:10, 11	KJV
125	251	SS.	4:7	" "
	252	SS.	1:15, 16	" "
	253	SS.	5:2	" "
127	254	Psal.	27:8	KJV
	255	" "	27:9	" "
	256	Psal.	63:6	KJV
	257	John	1:48	" "
	258	Dan.	6:10	" "
	259	Dan.	9:23	" "
130	260	Acts	1:9-11	KJV
	261	Acts	1:7	" "
	262	Matt.	24:27	KJV
	263	" "	24:30, 31	" "
131	264	" "	26:64	" "
	265	Mark	13:26, 27	" "
	266	" "	13:35, 36	" "
	267	" "	14:62	" "
	268	Luk.	21:26-28	" "
	269	I Cor.	15:23, 24	KJV
	270	I Thess.	2:19, 20	" "
132	271	" "	3:13	" "
	272	" "	4:16	" "
	273	James	5:7	" "
	274	I John	2:28	" "
	275	Rev.	21:2-5	" "
	276	Coloss.	3:3	" "
133	277	Heb.	10:30	KJV
	278	Acts	24:15	" "
	279	Psal.	90:3	" "

Page No.	SI. No.	Book Ref.	Chapter & Verse	Bible Version
133	280	Ezeki.	37:1-14	" "
135	281	John	5:28, 29	" "
	282	Luk.	20:34-37	KJV
136	283	I Cor.	15:50-55	" "
	284	I Thess.	4:16, 17	" "
137	285	I Cor.	15:42-44	KJV
	286	I Cor.	15:49	" "
	287	" "	15:35-38	GNB
138	288	" "	15:20-24	KJV
	289	I Cor.	15:45-49	KJV
	290	Matt.	22:30	KJV
139	291	I Thess.	4:16, 17	" "
	292	Ephes.	1:7	" "
141	293	John	20:19, 20	KJV
	294	Luk	24:30, 31	KJV
	295	John	20:27	" "
142	296	I Cor.	15:49	" "
	297	Isaiah	54:5	" "
	298	" "	61:10	" "
143	299	Heb.	9:27	KJV
	300	Rom.	14:10	" "
	301	Matt.	12:36	" "
	302	Acts.	7:6	" "
144	303	Rom.	2:6	KJV
	304	" "	3:24, 27,28	" "
	305	" "	3:24	" "
	306	" "	3:27	" "
	307	" "	3:28	" "
	308	I Timo.	5:24, 25	" "
	309	II Thes.	1:7-9	GNB
145	310	John	5:24	KJV
146	311	Rev.	7:17	KJV
	312	" "	21:4	" "
	313	I Cor.	4:5	" "
	314	Rom.	8:1	" "
	315	John	5:22, 23	" "
	316	" "	5:26, 27	" "

Page No.	SI. No.	Book Ref.	Chapter & Verse	Bible Version
146	317	Heb.	2:18	" "
	318	Heb.	4:15	KJV
147	319	Rom.	5:14	GNB
	320	" "	5:15	" "
	321	" "	5:16	" "
	322	" "	5:17	" "
	323	" "	5:18	" "
148	324	" "	5:19	" "
	325	John	5:24	KJV
149	326	Rom.	5:16	GNB
	327	II Cor.	5:17	KJV
	328	Luk.	11:13	" "
	329	Rom.	11:33	KJV
	330	I John	4:16	" "
150	331	I John	2:5, 6	KJV
	332	" "	2:24	" "
	333	" "	2:28	" "
	334	Philippi.	2:5	" "
151	335	John	14:23	" "
	336	I John	5:1	KJV
152	337	" "	3:14	" "
	338	" "	4:8	" "
	339	" "	4:20	" "
	340	Matt.	5:44	" "
	341	" "	5:7	" "
	342	James	2:13	" "
	343	I John	3:17	GNB
	344	" "	3:18	" "
155	345	Psal.	9:17	KJV
	346	Prov.	15:24	" "
156	347	Matt.	18:10	" "
	348	Job	1:9, 10	" "
157	349	Rev.	20:12	" "
	350	Matt.	6:24	" "
	351	" "	12:36	" "
	352	" "	5:28	" "
	353	Psal.	139:2	" "
	354	Rom.	3:10	
	355	II Pet.	2:10, 11	" "

Page No.	Sl. No.	Book Ref.	Chapter & Verse	Bible Version
158	356	Rom.	2:12	" "
	357	Heb.	10:26, 27	KJV
159	358	Mark	9:48	" "
	359	Rom.	13:14	" "
	360	" "	2:11	GNB
	361	Rom.	2:13-16	KJV
161	362	I Timo.	1:13	KJV
	363	I Pet.	3:8-19	" "
	364	" "	3:20, 21	" "
	365	Rom.	9:15	GNB
162	366	" "	9:15, 16	" "
	367	Rev.	1:18	KJV
163	368	Luk	16:19-25	" "
	369	Psal.	49:15	KJV
	370	Luk.	12:47, 48	GNB
165	371	John	10:11	KJV
	372	Heb.	13:20	" "
	373	I Pet.	2:25	KJV
	374	" "	5:4	" "
	375	Ephes.	4:7	" "
	376	" "	4:8	" "
	377	" "	4:9	" "
	378	Rev.	1:18	" "
	379	Rom.	5:8	GNB
	380	" "	5:10	" "
167	381	John	6:44	KJV
168	382	Luke	16:23-26	" "
	383	John	6:37	" "
	384	Luk	2:11	" "
	385	Matt.	2:1	" "
	386	" "	2:2	" "
169	387	Dan.	12:3	KJV
	388	I Cor.	15:41	" "
170	389	James	2:22-24	" "
	390	II Cor.	5:10	" "
	391	Matt.	13:43	" "
	392	Rom.	2:11	GNB
171	393	Luk.	15:22	KJV
	394	Rev.	19:8	" "
172	395	James	2:24	GNB
	396	Matt.	22:8	KJV
	397	Matt.	22:11-13	GNB
173	398	" "	5:48	" "
	399	Isaiah	42:3	KJV
	400	Matt.	12:20	" "
	401	Matt.	25:10	GNB
174	402	Matt.	25:13	KJV
	403	Mark	5:2-13	GNB
	404	James	2:19, 20	" "
	405	" "	2:17	KJV
	406	James	2:24	" "
175	407	I Cor.	2:9	" "
	408	Matt.	5:8	" "
176	409	John	14:1-3	KJV
	410	" "	14:5	" "
	411	" "	14:6	" "
	412	Rom.	8:34	KJV
177	413	Ephes.	4:8	GNB
	414	Matt.	7:21-23	KJV
	415	Luk.	11:13	" "
	416	John	14:26	" "
	417	Rom.	5:5	" "
	418	Matt.	25:34	GNB
178	419	Matt.	25:40	KJV
	420	" "	25:34-40	GNB
179	421	I Cor.	13 (full)	" "
180	422	Matt.	25:14-30	KJV
181	423	Matt.	18:3	GNB
182	424	Mark	9:44	KJV
183	425	Matt.	25:41-46	GNB
	426	Luk.	16:19	KJV
184	427	Prov.	7:22, 23	GNB
	428	Matt.	23:33	KJV
185	429	" "	23:34-36	KJV
186	430	John	3:16	" "
	431	Rom.	6:23	" "

Page No.	SI. No.	Book Ref.	Chapter & Verse	Bible Version
187	432	I Pet.	5:8	" "
	433	Matt.	13:43	" "
	434	Heb.	1:14	GNB
	435	John	1:12, 13	KJV
	436	Rom.	8:14	" "
188	437	I Cor.	6:3	" "
	438	Rom.	8:17	" "
	439	Matt.	6:9	" "
	440	I Cor.	13:12	" "
189	441	Matt.	22:37	GNB
	442	Mark	12:30, 33	" "
	443	Luke	10:27	" "
	444	Mark	12:33	KJV
	445	Matt	25:40	" "
	446	Rom.	13:10	" "
	447	Matt.	5:23, 24	" "
190	448	Mark	13:34, 36	KJV
	449	Luk.	12:35	" "
191	450	Luk.	12:37	" "
	451	Luk.	12:40	" "
	452	Mark	13:37	" "

Total: 452 Quotations from the Holy Bible.

Books from the Holy Bible referred indicating the relative abbreviations used in this book for reference.

Old Testament Books

Genesis	—	Gen.
Exodus	—	Exod.
Leviticus	—	Lev.
Deuteronomy	—	Deut.
Judges	—	Judg.
Ruth	—	Ruth
1 Samuel	—	I Sam.
2 Samuel	—	II Sam.
Job	—	Job
Psalms	—	Psal.
Proverbs	—	Prov.
Song of Songs	—	SS.

Isaiah	—	Isaiah
Ezekiel	—	Ezeki.
Daniel	—	Dan.

Apocripha Books

2 Maccabees	—	II Maccab.

New Testament Books

Matthews	—	Matt.
Marks	—	Mark.
Luke	—	Luk.
John	—	John
Acts	—	Acts
Romans	—	Rom.
1 Corinthians	—	I Cor.
2 Corinthians	—	II Cor.
Galatians	—	Gal.
Ephessians	—	Ephess.
Philippians	—	Philippi.
Colossians	—	Coloss.
1 Thessalonians	—	I Thess.
2 Thessalonians	—	II Thess.
1 Timothy	—	I Timo.
Hebrews	—	Heb.
James	—	James
1 Peter	—	I Pet.
2 Peter	—	II Pet.
1 John	—	I John
Revelations	—	Rev.

Note: This compendium of the quotations from the Holy Bible cited in the book *Glorious Life After Death,* is sufficient proof for the authenticity of the facts stated therein. I have referred several editions of the Holy Bible as I could afford to get in my limitations. Among them I found the two editions viz. the *King James Reference Edition* which is indicated in the abbreviation "KJV" and the *Good News Bible* which is indicated in the abbreviation "GNB," are more clear in expression. Even among these two I have preferred the one which was found to be more clear in expression in the particular contexts for explanation and understanding. Hope this will be of good guidance to the readers for referring to the Holy Bible while reading this book.

Author

Bibliography

The Holy Bible, Reference throughout the book in all chapters.

Book-*Life After Life,* by Ronald A. Moody Jr. M.D. with a foreword by Elizabeth Ross. M.D., published by arrangement with Mockingbird Books — 1975, references in Chapters 3 & 4.

Book-*You Live After Death* by Harold Sherman, published by Ballantine Books in 1949, references in Chapters 3 & 4.

Book-*The Four Last Things* — "Death, Judgement, Heaven, and Hell by Rev. Ronald J. Shell, M.A., B.sc., (of Brixton Independent Church), printed by W. Cave & Co. Brixton, London, reference in Chapter 1 & 9.

Book-*Psi* — "A Study of Psi Phenomena," by P. Vinodson, M.A., published by Jyothi Book House, Kottayam, 1981, reference in Chapter 2.

Book-*Voices from the Edge of Eternity,* compiled by John Myers & published by Pyramid Publication by Fleming H. Revell Company, Old Tappan, New Jersey, 07675, USA, 1968, reference in Chapter 2.

Magazine-*Readers Digest,* Article from October 2003 Issue, reference in Chapter 4.

Minni Maranja Jyothis (Malayalam Language) Biography of Yoohanon Mar Athanasios Metropolitan by Varghese Mathew, Karackatukuzhi, Kottayam, Chapter 1.

Book-*With Christ in the School of Prayer,* by Andrew Murray, Nisbet & Co. Ltd., Chapter 6, 22 Berners Street, London W. 1.

Kathopaniṣad, English Version by Swamy Chinmayananda, 1963.

The *Bhagavad-Gītā.*

The International Bible Commentary (Theological Publications In India)

Divine Harmony by Aravindāksha Menon, Chapter 6.

"*Introduction to the Bhagavad Gītā*" by Swami Chidbhavānanda Thapovan Publishing House, Tirupparaittuarai P.O., Tamil Nadu.

Index